Praise for

LATE MIGRATIONS

"A book that will be treasured." —*Minneapolis Star Tribune*

"What book would I want to see included on summer-reading tables everywhere? . . . A book of nonfiction by Margaret Renkl called *Late Migrations* that examines a quiet life through the lens of family and the natural world. I don't say this lightly, but [it] deserve[s] to be read for as long as kids have been reading *Of Mice and Men*." —ANN PATCHETT, *Wall Street Journal*

"A close and vigilant witness to loss and gain, Renkl wrenches meaning from the intimate moments that define us. Her work is a chronicle of being. And a challenge to cynicism. *Late Migrations* is flat-out brilliant and it has arrived right on time." —JOHN T. EDGE, author of *The Potlikker Papers*

"One of the best books I've read in a long time . . . [and] one of the most beautiful essay collections that I have ever read. It will give you chills." —SILAS HOUSE, author of *Southernmost*

"In her poignant debut, a memoir, Renkl weaves together observations from her current home in Nashville and short vignettes of nature and growing up in the South." —*Garden & Gun*

"*Late Migrations* has echoes of Annie Dillard's *The Writing Life*—with grandparents, sons, dogs and birds sharing the spotlight, it's a witty, warm and unaccountably soothing all-American story." —*People*

"This is the story of grief accelerated by beauty and beauty made richer by grief. . . . Like Patti Smith in *Woolgathering*, Renkl aligns natural history with personal history so completely that the one becomes the other. Like Annie Dillard in *Pilgrim at Tinker Creek*, Renkl makes, of a ring of suburbia, an alchemical exotica." —*The Rumpus*

"Renkl holds my attention with essays about plants and caterpillars in a way no other nature writer can." —MARY LAURA PHILPOTT, author of *I Miss You When I Blink*

"Gracefully written and closely observed, Renkl's lovely essays are tinged with the longing for family and places now gone while rejoicing in the flutter of birds and life still alive." —ALAN LIGHTMAN, author of *Einstein's Dreams*

"Here is an extraordinary mind combined with a poet's soul to register our own old world in a way we have not quite seen before. *Late Migrations* is the psychological and spiritual portrait of an entire family and place presented in quick takes—snapshots—a soul's true memoir. The dire dreams and fears of childhood, the mother's mysterious tears, the imperfect beloved family ... all are part of a charged and vibrant natural world also filled with rivalry, conflict, the occasional resolution, loss, and delight. *Late Migrations* is a continual revelation." —LEE SMITH, author of *The Last Girls*

"Renkl feels the lives and struggles of each creature that enters her yard as keenly as she feels the paths followed by her mother, grandmother, her people. Learning to accept the sometimes harsh, always lush natural world may crack open a window to acceptance of our own losses. In *Late Migrations*, we welcome new life, mourn its passing, and honor it along the way." —Indie Next List (July 2019), selected by KAT BAIRD, The Book Bin

"[A] stunning collection of essays merging the natural landscapes of Alabama and Tennessee with generations of family history, grief and renewal. Renkl's voice sounds very close to the reader's ear: intimate, confiding, candid and alert." —*Shelf Awareness* (starred review)

"How can any brief description capture this entirely original and deeply satisfying book? . . . I can't help but compile a list of people I want to gift with *Late Migrations*. I want them to emerge from it, as I did, ready to apprehend the world freshly, better able to perceive its connections and absorb its lessons." —*Chapter 16*

"Like the spirituality of Krista Tippett's *On Being* meets the brevity of Joe Brainard . . . The miniature essays in *Late Migrations* approach with modesty, deliver bittersweet epiphanies, and feel like small doses of religion." —*Literary Hub*

"[A] magnificent debut . . . Renkl instructs that even amid life's most devastating moments, there are reasons for hope and celebration. Readers will savor each page and the many gems of wisdom they contain." —*Publishers Weekly* (starred review)

"Compelling, rich, satisfying . . . The short, potent essays of Renkl's *Late Migrations* are objects as worthy of marvel and study as the birds and other creatures they observe." —*Foreword Reviews* (starred review)

"A melding of flora, fauna and family . . . Renkl captures the spirit and contemporary culture of the American South better than anyone." —*Book Page* (A 2019 Most Anticipated Nonfiction Book)

"[*Late Migrations*] is shot through with deep wonder and a profound sense of loss. It is a fine feat, this book. Renkl intimately knows that 'this life thrives on death' and chooses to sing the glory of being alive all the same." —*Booklist*

LATE
MIGRATIONS

LATE MIGRATIONS

A Natural History of Love and Loss

Margaret Renkl

With art by

Billy Renkl

MILKWEED EDITIONS

Published 2019 by Milkweed Editions
Printed in Canada
Cover design by Mary Austin Speaker
Cover art by Billy Renkl
19 20 21 22 23 5 4 3
First Edition

Milkweed Editions, an independent nonprofit publisher, gratefully acknowledges sustaining support from the Ballard Spahr Foundation; the Jerome Foundation; the McKnight Foundation; the National Endowment for the Arts; the Target Foundation; and other generous contributions from foundations, corporations, and individuals. Also, this activity is made possible by the voters of Minnesota through a Minnesota State Arts Board Operating Support grant, thanks to a legislative appropriation from the arts and cultural heritage fund. For a full listing of Milkweed Editions supporters, please visit milkweed.org.

Library of Congress Cataloging-in-Publication Data

Names: Renkl, Margaret, author. | Renkl, Billy, illustrator.
Title: Late migrations : a natural history of love and loss / Margaret Renkl ; with art by Billy Renkl.
Description: First edition. | Minneapolis : Milkweed Editions, 2019.
Identifiers: LCCN 2018044003 (print) | LCCN 2018057281 (ebook) | ISBN 9781571319876 (ebook) | ISBN 9781571313782 (hardcover : alk. paper)
Subjects: LCSH: Renkl, Margaret. | Renkl, Margaret—Family. | Journalists—United States—Biography. | Adult children of aging parents—United States—Biography.
Classification: LCC PN4874.R425 (ebook) | LCC PN4874.R425 A3 2019 (print) |
    DDC 818/.603 [B]—dc23
LC record available at https://lccn.loc.gov/2018044003

Milkweed Editions is committed to ecological stewardship. We strive to align our book production practices with this principle, and to reduce the impact of our operations in the environment. We are a member of the Green Press Initiative, a nonprofit coalition of publishers, manufacturers, and authors working to protect the world's endangered forests and conserve natural resources. *Late Migrations* was printed on acid-free 100% postconsumer-waste paper by Friesens Corporation.

For my family

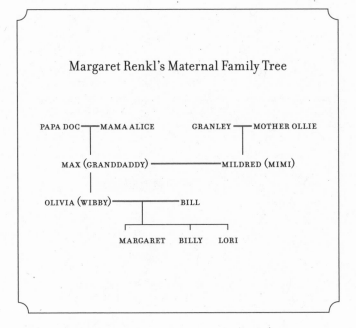

Margaret Renkl's Maternal Family Tree

PAPA DOC ─┬─ MAMA ALICE   GRANLEY ─┬─ MOTHER OLLIE
          │   │
   MAX (GRANDDADDY) ──────────── MILDRED (MIMI)
          │
OLIVIA (WIBBY) ─────┬───── BILL
                    │
        ┌───────────┼───────────┐
    MARGARET   BILLY   LORI

Well, dear, life is a casting off. It's always that way.

ARTHUR MILLER, *DEATH OF A SALESMAN*

Therefore all poems are elegies.

GEORGE BARKER

LATE
MIGRATIONS

PEACH

In Which My Grandmother Tells the Story

of My Mother's Birth

We didn't expect her quite as early as she came. We were at Mother's peeling peaches to can. Daddy had several peach trees, and they had already canned some, and so we were canning for me and Max. And all along as I would peel I was eating, so that night around twelve o'clock I woke up and said, "Max, my stomach is hurting so much I just can't stand it hardly. I must have eaten too many of those peaches."

And so once in a while, you see, it would just get worse; then it would get better.

We didn't wake Mother, but as soon as Max heard her up, he went in to tell her. And she said, "Oh, Max, go get your daddy right now!" Max's daddy was the doctor for all the folks around here.

While he was gone she fixed the bed for me, put on clean sheets and fixed it for me. Mama Alice came back with him too—Mama Alice and Papa Doc. So they were both with me, my mother on one side and Max's on the other, and they were holding my hands. And Olivia was born around twelve o'clock that day. I don't know the time exactly.

Max was in and out, but they said Daddy was walking around the house, around and around the house. He'd stop every now and then and find out what was going on. And when she was born, it was real quick. Papa Doc jerked up, and he said, "It's a girl," and Max said, "Olivia."

Red in Beak and Claw

The first year, a day before the baby bluebirds were due to hatch, I checked the nest box just outside my office window and found a pinprick in one of the eggs. Believing it must be the pip that signals the beginnings of a hatch, I quietly closed the box and resolved not to check again right away, though the itch to peek was nearly unbearable: I'd been waiting years for a family of bluebirds to take up residence in that box, and finally an egg was about to shudder and pop open. Two days later, I realized I hadn't seen either parent in some time, so I checked again and found all five eggs missing. The nest was undisturbed.

The cycle of life might as well be called the cycle of death: everything that lives will die, and everything that dies will be eaten. Bluebirds eat insects; snakes eat bluebirds; hawks eat snakes; owls eat hawks. That's how wildness works, and I know it. I was heartbroken anyway.

I called the North American Bluebird Society for advice, just in case the pair returned for a second try. The guy who answered the help line thought perhaps my bluebirds—not "mine," of course, but the bluebirds I loved—had been attacked by both a house wren and a snake. House wrens are furiously territorial and will attempt to disrupt the nesting of any birds nearby. They fill unused nest holes with sticks to prevent competitors from settling there; they destroy unprotected nests and pierce all the eggs; they have been known to kill nestlings and even brooding females. Snakes simply swallow the eggs whole, slowly and gently, leaving behind an intact nest.

The bluebird expert recommended that I install a wider

snake baffle on the mounting pole and clear out some brush that might be harboring wrens. If the bluebirds returned, he said, I should install a wren guard over the hole as soon as the first egg appeared: the parents weren't likely to abandon an egg, and disguising the nest hole with a cover might keep wrens from noticing it. I bought a new baffle, but the bluebirds never came back.

The next year another pair took up residence. After the first egg appeared, I went to the local bird supply store and asked for help choosing a wren guard, but the store didn't stock them; house wrens don't nest in Middle Tennessee, the owner said. I know they aren't *supposed* to nest here, I said, but listen to what happened last year. He scoffed: possibly a migrating wren had noticed the nest and made a desultory effort to destroy it, but there are no house wrens nesting in Middle Tennessee. All four bluebird eggs hatched that year, and all four bluebird babies safely fledged, so I figured he must know this region better than the people at the bluebird society, and I gave no more thought to wren guards.

The year after that, there were no bluebirds. Very early in February, long before nesting season, a male spent a few minutes investigating the box, but he never returned with a female. Even the chickadees, who nest early and have always liked our bluebird box, settled for the box under the eaves near the back door. All spring, the bluebird box sat empty.

Then I started to hear the unmistakable sound of a house wren calling for a mate. Desperately the wren would call and call and then spend some time filling the box with sticks, building an elaborate scaffolding that formed a deep tunnel running across the top of the box and down to its very floor. Day after day: singing, sticks, singing, sticks. The side yard was his exclusive domain. No longer did the chickadees visit the mealworm feeder on that side of the house; the goldfinches abandoned the thistle feeder nearby; only the largest birds dared drink from the birdbath. I set another dish of water on the other side of the house because we'd had so little rain.

Meanwhile, the chickadees hatched out a magnificent brood of babies. Their voices were full and strong, and their parents worked continually from sunup till dark feeding them. After they fledged, right on schedule, I took the box down for cleaning. At the bottom was one fully feathered baby, probably only minutes from leaving the box. It was dead from a puncture wound to the head.

It's one thing to recognize the bloodbath that is the natural world and a different thing entirely to participate in it. There's nothing "natural" about offering wild birds food and water and housing, even in an area where human beings have systematically destroyed their original nesting sites and food sources. With that invitation comes an obligation to protect and defend the creatures who accept it. Even before I found the dead chick, I had made up my mind to take down my nest boxes after the house wrens fledged, both to discourage the wren from returning and to keep from attracting other native cavity dwellers—tufted titmice, Carolina wrens—to house wren territory.

Thing is, I love the little brown wrens too. Their courtship song is one of the most beautiful in the world, a high, thin river made of musical notes tumbling and rushing and cascading downstream. And it's hard to fault them for doing only what millions of years of evolution have taught them to do, in their impossibly tiny fierceness, to survive a world of high winds and pelting rains and predators. To see that small brown bird lifting his throat to the sky and releasing that glorious sound into the world, again and again and again, day after day—how could it be possible not to root for him, not to hope a mate would arrive, in this region where house wrens don't nest, to accept him and his offering of sticks? When a female joined him ten days later, I had to cheer.

Then a blackberry winter descended on Middle Tennessee, and that night it was twenty degrees colder than the temperature a house wren egg needs to remain viable. The next morning, the goldfinches returned to the thistle feeder.

Let Us Pause to Consider What a Happy Ending Actually Looks Like

LOWER ALABAMA, 1936

In the story my grandmother told, there was an old woman of uncertain race who lived among them but did not belong. With no land and no way to grow anything, the old woman was poorer and more desolate than the others, and they looked the other way when she slipped into their barns after dark with her candle and her rucksack, intent on taking corn. Did a barn owl startle her that night? Did a mule jostle her arm? They never knew: she never admitted to being there. The howling fire took the barn whole and then roared to the house. Neighbors saved some of the furniture in a kind of bucket line, but an actual bucket line was impossible: the water tank had stood on a wooden scaffold already lost to the blaze. There was no time to save the clothes and quilts, the food my grandmother had stored for winter, the grain my grandfather had put up for his mules. Worst of all, there was no time to save the wild-eyed mules stamping in their stalls.

In my grandmother's story, they brought what the neighbors had salvaged to her in-laws' house half a mile down the road, and family came from every direction to resettle things, making room. The back porch became the room where Papa Doc and Mama Alice slept. The parlor became my grandparents' room. The nooks where my mother and her infant brother slept were upstairs, in what had been the attic.

Decades later, when my mother told stories of her girlhood,

she never seemed to recall how crowded the house must have been or how the tensions surely flared. Instead she remembered my great-grandparents' devotion. Every day Papa Doc would leave for calls with his black bag or, on slow mornings, head to the store to pick up the mail. When he came home again, he always called out, "Alice?" as soon as he reached their rose border. And she would always call back, formally, from the garden or the kitchen or the washtub on the porch, "I'm here, Dr. Weems."

My mother's grandparents went through the day in a kind of dance, preordained steps that took them away from each other—he to his rounds across the countryside, she to the closer world of clothesline and pea patch and barn—but brought them back together again and again, touching for just a moment before moving away once more.

But the shadow side of love is always loss, and grief is only love's own twin. My mother was twelve when Mama Alice died. Papa Doc sat down on the porch and settled there, staring at the rambling rosebushes growing beside the road. "He just made up his mind to die, I guess," my mother always said. "He lasted barely more than a month."

WATER LILY

Encroachers

The sun is setting on the lily pond, winking on the water between the floating circles of the lily pads, winking on the brown leaves caught on the green surface of the dense lilies. The wind is stirring the water, rippling the mirrored trees on the bank, and now the deep-red leaves of the sumac are falling too, and the yellow maples and the orange sassafras. Soon the pond will be covered over with lily pads and leaves. In only a little while—five years? ten? no more than a blink—the water will cease to echo these trees and this sky. Today the brown water is glowing in the autumn light, on fire with light and color and motion, but the pond is dying.

It is impossible to believe the pond is dying.

The lilies are choking it, starving it of light and oxygen. Soon there will be no room left for fish or frog or snake or turtle. There will be only lilies, lilies from edge to edge, a marsh of lilies where nothing else can live. In summer the lilies bloom—oh, how beautifully the lilies bloom, how fragrant their flowers!—and even now, at the very end of autumn at the very end of the day, the lovely pond is filled with light, encircled and embraced. Leaves resting on the lily pads, hawk floating overhead, rabbit crouching under the tree—all life piled on life—and still it is dying.

The pond is dying, and now I am thinking of starlings reeling through the sky at dusk, the glory of the starlings in motion, wheeling and dipping and rising as one black beast made of pulsing cells, as one creature born to live in air. But the starlings don't belong any more than the lilies belong; they are aliens here. This is not their sky. These are not their trees. They are robbing the dogwoods, leaving no berries for the mockingbirds. They have claimed every nest hole, leaving none for the titmice or the bluebirds or even the bossy chickadees.

The alien does not know it's an alien.

When a starling hangs itself at dawn on the wire holding up my peanut feeder, and I wake to find it dangling there, black and stiff and cold, I can only pity it, hungry and confused and now lost to the world. But a downy woodpecker, unconcerned by the specter hanging above its head, is finally getting its fill of peanuts.

In Which My Grandmother Tells the Story

of Her Favorite Dog

LOWER ALABAMA, 1940

I was still teaching when Max Junior and Olivia were in school. Our school was a very short distance from home, and we walked. Of course, I always walked by myself; they were always running and playing. And my dog, her name was Honey, always followed me, and she would get up under my desk and stay there as long as I was at my desk. If I went to the board, she went with me and laid down by my feet as long as I was writing on the board. One weekend she went missing, and we looked everywhere for her. We didn't find her until Monday morning. When we got to school, we smelled something, and it was this dog. She had crawled right up under the school building, right under where I sat. That's where she was when she died.

Howl

The old dog wakes when the door shuts fast. *Click* goes the back door, and *thump* goes the car door, and now the old dog believes he is alone in the house. When the whine of the car backing out of the drive gives way to the crunch of tires on the road, and then to silence, the old dog believes he is alone in the world. Standing next to the door, he folds himself up, lowering his hindquarters gradually, bit by bit, slowly, until his aching haunches have touched the floor. Now he slides his front feet forward, slowly, slowly, and he is down.

A moan begins in the back of his throat, lower pitched than a whine, higher than a groan, and grows. His head tips back. His eyes close. The moan escapes in a rush of vowels, louder and louder and louder, and now he is howling. It is the sound he made in his youth whenever an ambulance passed on the big road at the edge of the neighborhood, but he can't hear so far anymore. Now he is howling in despair. He is howling for his long life's lost companion, the dog who died last year and left him to sleep alone. He is howling for his crippled hips, so weak he can hardly squat to relieve himself. He is howling because it's his job to protect this house, but he is too old now to protect the house. He is howling because the world is empty, and he is howling because he is still here.

In Which My Grandmother Tells the Story

of the Day I Was Born

LOWER ALABAMA, 1961

O*n Mother's Day of 1961, Bill and Olivia came to our house, and Bill—this is the way he gave Olivia her gift—said, "This is to the sweetest little mother-to-be there is." That's the way he told us. And that was when she was going to have Margaret. And so we kept the road pretty hot between our house and yours after that. And when she was born, Bill called us and said he wanted me to go with him to Montgomery. They thought they would have to take Margaret up there. She was having the breathing trouble that that Kennedy child had later on, and he died. And so Max carried me down there, but when we got there, they had gotten it straightened out well enough that they thought it wouldn't be necessary to take her. So we stayed a few days, until Olivia could get up and was able to bathe the baby and look after her.*

To the Bluebirds

I know: there are too many dogs in the yard; and the giant house going up next door is too much hulking house lumbering too near the little nest box, never mind the beeping, growling trucks and the bellowing carpenters and the scrambling roofers with their machine-gun nails; and the miniature forest behind us still harbors agile-fingered raccoons and rat snakes as thick as my arm; and a Cooper's hawk still patrols the massive pine tree on the other side of the house.

But consider: the dogs are old and spend their time lying in the sun, their glad bird-chasing days long past. And the noisy builders, too close now in house-scouting season, will be gone by nesting time, replaced by neighbors who will drive straight into their garage, never lingering in what's left of their yard. Look at the predator baffle, much larger than last year's, and the now-bare ground where before the brush sheltered house wrens.

Look: see the sturdy birdbath I've moved to your side of the yard, and the special feeder designed to hold live mealworms? The greatest token of my love for you is that every day now I reach into a mesh bag full of live mealworms and pluck them out, one by one, and drop them into the ceramic cup in the feeder. The worms stay in my refrigerator, where the cool darkness is meant to keep them in a state of dormancy, but oh my God they are not dormant. No, they curl their segmented bodies around my finger, and they lift their nubby heads and rebuke me with their nonexistent eyes, but I harden my heart to their plight and plink them into that little white cup, and I walk away as they twist and curl around each other in search of purchase. They are my gift to you on these cold days when nary a cricket stirs in the dry grass.

The Way You Looked at Me

Here are all my kin—my mother and my father, my grand-mother and my grandfather, my great-grandmother in the placid wholeness of her white halo—arrayed around me. Born too early, tiny and frail, I am sleeping in every picture, and in every picture they are gathered around me, heads bent to watch me take each too-light breath, willing my lips not to turn blue again. I am too small and always cold, but my people are looking at me as if I were the sun. My parents and my grand-parents and my great-grandmother, all of them, have gathered to watch over me. They are looking at me as if I were the sun, as if they had been cold every day of their lives until now.

I am the sun, but they are not the planets.

They are the universe.

Not Always in the Sky

Our neighborhood is home to a very large red-tailed hawk. The hawk's telltale color is muted in females, in certain lights almost brown, and the dead tree this hawk often uses as a hunting perch is distant enough from the street to make the bird's identity a matter for debate. My neighbors are convinced this bird is an eagle.

"Go home and get your camera!" one stops her car to say as I walk the dog. "There's an eagle in the dead tree!" I go home and get the camera, just to be safe, but the dog and I have just passed the dead tree, and perched in it was a large red-tailed hawk. When I go back with my camera, she is still there.

There's much talk here about the eagle who has taken up residence in our neighborhood, but no one seems to wonder what kind of eagle it might be. When I first heard the rumors, I thought perhaps my neighbors were seeing a young bald eagle. Everyone knows an adult bald eagle on sight, but juveniles always pose a challenge in birds. There was a remote possibility, too, of a visit by a golden eagle, a species generally found west of the Mississippi but reintroduced in Tennessee not long ago; several birds equipped with transmitters are known to spend winter on the Cumberland Plateau. But only by the most muscular effort of imagination could this bird be a golden eagle. We don't live on the Cumberland Plateau.

The bird is clearly a red-tailed hawk, but I don't say anything to my neighbors. People want to believe that something extraordinary has happened to them, that they have been singled out for grace, and who am I to rob them of one sheen of enchantment still available in the first-ring suburbs?

Working at my desk one day, I hear a great mob of blue jays sounding the alarm: a predator is in their midst. Minutes pass, and their rage shows no signs of dissipating, so I step outside. Perhaps the hawk that looks like an eagle has landed in my own yard.

But I see nothing in the sky, nothing in the trees, nothing on the utility pole at the corner of the yard, nothing on the power lines. And then I notice that the blue jays are looking down as they scream out their jeering cry of warning, and that all the smaller birds, even the ground foragers, have taken to the bushes and the honeysuckle tangles and are looking downward too. The little Cooper's hawk who hunts in this yard will often stand on his prey for a bit, working to get a better grip on his struggling victim before taking to the sky, but there is no hawk on the ground either.

Walking farther into the yard, I still don't see anything, even scanning the ground with a zoom lens. And then it dawns on me that the birds must be looking at a snake. This lot backs up to a city easement, only a few yards wide, that leads from the wooded area behind our neighbor's house out to the side street next to ours. We leave the easement untended, and the part of our yard that abuts it as well, because it serves as a kind of wildlife corridor. A very large rat snake, at least five feet long, hunts under our house and all over this yard, but I wouldn't be able to see it in the easement unless I was practically upon it. I walk a little closer but only a little. Though I am not especially afraid of snakes, I know they are afraid of me, and I like to give them their room.

Holding a useless camera, I suddenly realize that something extraordinary is happening right before me, a great serpent slowly on the move and all the songbirds aware of its presence and calling to each other and telling each other to beware. The miracle isn't happening in the sky at all. It's happening in the damp weeds of an ordinary backyard, among last year's moldering leaves and the fragrant soil turned up by moles.

Blood Kin

In the picture I'm dressed entirely in white: white dress with puffed sleeves, white bonnet with white lace around the brim, white tights and white polished high-tops, the kind all babies wore. It must be an Easter picture, you think, because what parent would dress a toddler in white more than once a year? But it can't be Easter. My grandmother, who's holding me in her lap on the porch steps, and my great-grandmother beside her, each with a halo of white hair that matches my frothy bonnet, are wearing dark dresses. And no farm woman in Alabama would be caught dead wearing navy blue on the day of the Resurrection.

The picture's off-center; there's room for my mother beside my great-grandmother, but Mama is perched on the next step up, smiling behind us, a little out of focus from the shift in depth of field. She's hiding because my brother will be born in April, and she always hid from cameras when she was pregnant.

Never mind that birth and death were entirely unremarkable in the world of that photo. Every chicken she ate with dumplings was one whose neck her grandmother had wrung. Every Christmas ham was once a piglet in her yard. All the babies in that county were born in their parents' beds and too often died there as well. The cemetery is full of tiny graves whose headstones are carved with terrible phrases: "Many fond hopes lie buried here." "Another jewel for the Maker's crown."

My grandmother's third child was born too soon, so early he had no name. She never told anyone else about him, but she told me, years later, when I could not stop weeping after my own miscarriages: "I had him in the chamber pot on the floor next to the bed," she said. "Nights I cried for a long time after that. Days I went to work like always."

Nests

Oblivion would be easier—not to know when the rat snake noses aside the tangle of grasses the cottontail has carefully patted into place, not to see it lift the impossibly soft fur she has plucked from her own belly, not to fathom that it is slowly, almost mechanically, swallowing the blind babies she has borne for just this moment.

Better not to discover that a still brown cardinal is sitting on two speckled eggs in the hollow of the holly beside the fence, her orange beak the only hint of her presence in the brown nest in the crook of the brown branches. Better not to hear the crow flapping down to the fencerow or to see its black head driving her from the holly with a single plunging probe through the leaves, or to understand that it is eating her eggs, indifferent to the driving sweeps of her furious mate and her own piteous calls.

Oh, to unsee the Carolina wren waiting so patiently in the tunnel of fronds she has wrapped around herself deep in the potted fern, invisible, but not invisible to the side-eyed jay. Oh, to unwatch her disbelief as she hops around and around the edge of the flowerpot, searching in vain for a hungry mouth to open for the caterpillar she has brought.

Scolding will not save the little sac of mantis eggs the neighborhood boys are batting around like a ball, or the spider's web swept from the eaves by a homeowner's broom, or the cluster of frog eggs at the edge of the pond where the newt is hunting.

This life thrives on death.

But hold very, very still in the springtime sun, and a tufted titmouse will come to harvest your hair and spin it into a soft, warm place for her young. Keep an eye on the ivy climbing the side of the house, and one day you will see a pair of finches coaxing their babies from a tiny nest balanced among the leaves. Hear the bluebirds calling from the trees, and you might turn in time to see a fledgling peer from the hole in the dark nest box, gape at the bright wide world for the very first time, and then trust itself to the sky. Wait at the window on the proper day, and the cottontail nest hidden under the rosemary bush will open before you, spilling forth little rabbits who lift the leaves from last fall and push aside their mother's fur and raise their ears and wrinkle their noses and bend for their first taste of the bitter dandelion. And it will be exactly what they wanted.

THUNDERSTORM

In the Storm, Safe from the Storm

LOWER ALABAMA, 1965

At my grandparents' house in the country, we live on the front porch, where the ceiling fan blows the bugs away and stirs the steaming air into something passing for a breeze. At home in town we are very modern and have no porch at all. There's a concrete stoop but only the barest overhang to cover it, hardly anything to keep away the rain or the blistering sun. When a storm comes, my father sets his chair right in the doorway, straddling the jamb. I love the storms. If I'm asleep, he lifts me up and carries me through the dark house to sit with him in the doorway and listen to the wind and the thunder.

The rain comes and I feel it with the tips of my toes, but they are the only parts of me that get wet, for I have drawn my knees up to my chest under my nightgown, and my father has unbuttoned his corduroy jacket and pulled it around me, and wrapped his arms around me too. I lean into him. I feel the heat from his body and the cool rain from the world, both at once.

Secret

Wild storms always come to Tennessee in the spring-time. One year a wind shear hit a hackberry tree three doors down from us and snapped it off right at the middle. The crown of the tree came down hard in seventy-mile-an-hour winds, taking out a maple and several large cypresses and crashing through a length of cedar fencing, barely missing the next-door neighbors' car.

That night the local news was full of trees that had in fact smashed into cars, but the scene here was even more dramatic. The tragic hackberry, it turned out, was completely hollow. And in that hollow lived approximately forty-five thousand wild honeybees, who came pouring out of the broken trunk the way they do in that scene in *Little House in the Big Woods* where Pa chases a bear away from a bee tree so he can harvest their honey for himself.

Here in suburbia, the homeowners were keeping a wary distance. Who knows how long those bees had been living in our midst, three steps from the street? And yet we'd pushed our strollers and walked our dogs past it every day without a single sting. Even so, the sight of forty-five thousand distraught honeybees pouring into the sky at once can be deeply unnerving. Someone called the Nashville Area Beekeepers Association, and the next morning an expert arrived. He was the one who estimated the size of the hive and captured the queen bee from the fallen part of the tree.

The queen was not hard to find, actually: she was surrounded by an entire army of worker bees who really did not want to share her. But the beeman in his thin shirtsleeves was not alarmed. He just reached in, scooped her up, and installed her in a commercial beehive that he had set next to the fallen tree. Then he gathered several dripping honeycombs and smeared them in and around the hollow to give the bees something to eat while they were looking for their queen.

It was a good plan, a nature-friendly plan to preserve a surprisingly healthy population of a crucial pollinator that's long been in trouble. Every time I took our old dog for a walk, I noticed the bees still pouring out of the standing part of the hackberry trunk, but they were also buzzing around the honey and the hivebox next to it too. Everything seemed to be going according to the brave beeman's plan.

But the wild honeybees, hidden safely from human eyes for so long, had devised their own plan according to an ancient logic that did not involve that hivebox on the ground. Two days later they had gathered in one of the remaining cypress trees: clinging to each other and crawling on top of each other, they formed a giant, roiling, ice-cream-cone-shaped swarm. The whole cypress was humming.

Then one of the scout bees must have returned with word of an acceptable site for a new hive—when I checked again at lunchtime, they were gone. The wind-ruined tree, the hackberry that had kept those honeybees a secret for at least a generation, was silent again.

Confirmation

My mother attended Mass at the little clapboard church for years before she formally joined it. Until then, she wasn't a full member of the congregation and did not receive Communion—she didn't want to upset her own father, the lifelong Methodist. Tucked away in a remote corner of southeast Alabama, my grandfather had never laid eyes on a Catholic before he met his future son-in-law.

The day before the wedding, one of the retired farmers who gathered on the Holsum Bread bench outside the community store had some news for my grandfather: the priest who performed the wedding ceremony would also mount my mother that very night. Hadn't anyone mentioned it? It was a Catholic rule, the old farmer said. The bride must sleep with the priest the night before the wedding to confirm that everything was in working order, to be sure that other crossbacks would appear in due time.

In his wisdom, my grandfather said nothing. Only when my mother was confirmed into my father's church did my grandfather confess the terrible story he'd heard. He hadn't believed it, he said, and anyhow he was relieved she had finally seen her way to becoming Catholic: "I didn't want to say a word, daughter, but a woman belongs in her husband's church."

The Parable of the Fox and the Chicken

The plain yellow chicken stalks the green sward with the other plain yellow chickens and a few baroque brown ones with curling feathers and arching necks. Moving through the grass, they fan out across garden and pasture and compost pile, pausing to warm their reptile feet in its heat. They work tirelessly, clearing stubble and stalk of every small crawling thing too slow for their sharp black eyes and scratching pink toes.

Their eyes cast down, they do not see the fox step out of the trees at the edge of the wood, but the mares see. They push their velvet noses under the pasture fence to watch as the ragged fox pounces. The bird is fat, but perhaps the fox is young; the horses gaze, rapt, upon a struggle that should not be a struggle. The other chickens hasten on heavy wings away, away—up the hill, down the hill, into the low branches of the very trees that sheltered the fox—with no thought of their stricken sister or her shrieking cries or her fruitlessly beating wings.

The barn cat, hardly bigger than a yellow chicken, becomes the unlikely hero of this tale, entering the fray and driving the feckless fox back into the trees. But the cat does not exult in her triumph. The mares do not gaze at each other in amazement. The chicken is not grateful for her rescue. She is hurt but not mortally hurt. A day or two in the safety of the coop, and she will be fine.

Or she would be fine but for her sisters, who cannot, will not, leave her alone. On this hill there is a pecking order, and it is not a metaphor. The hens, not the fox, are now her enemies, the plain yellow chickens and the ornate brown ones alike. She cannot live safely alone, and she cannot live safely with her flock. The hands that fling the corn will dress her for supper, and the fox will go hungry tonight.

The Monster in the Window

The ceiling was sloped in my mother's childhood bedroom, all angles and lines in a sanctuary carved from half the attic. Even the attic itself was an afterthought, added willy-nilly to a peg-built dogtrot: two rooms connected by a breezeway, the only kind of house that makes sense in the oppressive heat of Lower Alabama. By the time my mother came to live there as a child, it had doors, four more rooms, and two attic nooks: one for her and one for her younger brother. Decades later, my own brother and I slept there when she was sick.

The stairs and the walls of that makeshift old house were covered with dark pine boards, and neither the staircase nor the landing was lighted. Climbing the steep steps to sleep alone in those close rooms felt like walking upstairs into a basement, ascending into an underworld. In summer the heat must have been suffocating, but I don't recall the sticky sheets or the hair clinging to the back of my neck or the restless turning all night long. What looms in memory is the fan at the top of the stairs. Built into the huge dormer window on the landing between the bedrooms, it faced out into a damp, bat-blasted night, a vast machine the size of an airplane propeller that pulled air from the screen doors through the still house and up the stairs. There was nothing, no screen or wire cage, between the spinning blades and a little girl's hand. My grandmother told me it would cut off my arm if I tried to touch it.

I never did, was never even tempted to, but at night I would lie in bed and listen to that fan, its roar drowning out the night-singing insects and the crunching tires as my father turned the family car from the dirt yard onto the blacktop, carrying my weeping mother into a blacker night than the one that enveloped our own house in town. I didn't hear them leave. I was listening to the terrible fan, afraid some larger force, something cold and inexplicable, might make me lean into those spinning blades and find myself sucked through and cast by bits into the black, fathomless sky.

When I could bear the darkness no longer, I would pull a string to light the single bulb in the closet. Thumbtacked to the narrow door were the curling tatters of my mother's old life, the life before me, the life before my father: 4-H ribbons and funeral-parlor fans and wedding announcements and corsages with petals turned to powder. I loved especially all the photos of my mother before she was my mother. In one she's posed on the grass, her waist surrounded by the full circle of a chiffon skirt: my mother the daisy, my mother the medallion. In another she's sitting on a low stone wall, the very center in a line of girls in pale dresses, all of them smiling and squinting into the sun.

When did she stop smiling? When did her dresses cease to sprawl so extravagantly across the jeweled grass? I always wondered. At home she would lie in her room with the curtains drawn on long, long Sunday afternoons, but I liked to imagine this other mother, this movie-star mother in the dancing dress with a flower tied to her wrist and a careless smile. That girl did not yet know there was a monster in the window, one that could chew her up and send her out into the night in pieces.

The Snow Moon

Here in this first-ring suburban neighborhood, we are far from the spongy paths of the forest peoples who gave this moon its name, but we are not far from the snow moon itself, which rises through the bare trees as it has done since long before we were here, since long before the forest peoples were here. The world is warming now, and this year the snow moon heralds no snow: the bluebirds are peeking into the sun-drenched nest box, the star magnolia is in full bloom weeks before its time, but still the snow moon rises between the black branches in our postage-stamp yards, as lovely as it has ever been, untouched by all our rancor, unmoved by our despair.

Let the earth cast a shadow across its golden glow. Let the green-headed comet streak past, unclasped, on its journey through the darkness. Still the snow moon rises and sets as it must. It has never burned, and it will never darken: all its light is borrowed light. Its steadfast path is tied to ours. The snow moon brought a time of hunger to the forest peoples, but we are fat in our snug houses, tethered to the shine of our screens. The snow moon is our hungry sister. The snow moon is our brighter twin.

Swept Away

For eighteen years, no one came to the front door of our house in Tennessee but local politicians and trick-or-treaters and teenagers selling magazines. The brick path was slick with moss and buckled by the roots of maple trees, and guests rarely chanced it. Better to follow the driveway around the house and take the stairs to the back door.

My husband's frail parents forced the issue, and we finally replaced the crumbling bricks with scored cement. I am in love with the jaunty stripes of monkey grass along the outside edge, and the solid place to squat as I weed the flower bed. I love to see it gleaming in the darkening light beneath the too-close trees, a welcoming path through the clover. As soon as the cement was safe to step on, I set to keeping it tidy. Left, left, left, I would swing the broom from the center out; then right, right, right, just the same. Left, left; right, right, and in a moment I'd cleared the windfall, put straight the gently curving track, brought to momentary order one bit of chaos.

And then one day: left, right, left, right, I'm swinging the broom like a metronome, like the pendulum of a grandfather clock. Left, right, and suddenly I am a tiny girl holding a broom too large for me, holding it halfway down the handle, dragging it too lightly across the footpath that leads from the road to my grandparents' house. My grandmother is saying, "Honey, swing it back and forth like this." Back and forth, left, right, she demonstrates, and I try, too, the bristles scraping the tops of my bare feet, the broomstick grazing the top of my head as

I bend to watch it whiff the air above the acorn crowns and the twigs and the brown petals from the blown roses and the crumbled bits of rock tracked in from the roadbed. Soon I am more or less copying my grandmother, making the motions my kin have made in this very place for four generations, back to when the path was hard-packed dirt.

Left, right, left, right, and now my grandmother is sitting on the swing in the dark, waiting for us on the porch as we drive down lonely county roads with never more than a single light shining in the towns—some not even towns, not even a crossroads where two blacktops come together in the middle of fields and fields and fields. Our grandmother rises and stands in the doorway while our weeping mother waits in the car, while our strong father lifts my brother and me from the back seat and carries us down the walk, across the porch, and up to the attic room where our mother slept as a girl, the room where my mother was happy as a girl. She is not always happy as a mother.

How long do I lie in the dark, listening? How long do I wait as that ancient house settles and sighs under immense trees that creak in the wind, to hear my father bringing my mother back to me from the long, dark highway? I wait and wait.

But when I turn over in bed, there are lights that glide like fairies across the wall between the shadows of leaves, and downstairs my grandmother is in the kitchen with Eola, who comes every day to help with the cooking and the housework and my ailing grandfather—Eola, who makes the lightest yeast rolls anywhere, and who once baked me a birthday cake like no other I had ever seen: a Barbie doll at the center of a hoop skirt made of frothy frosting. A Scarlett O'Hara cake made by the hands of a black woman who worked for a dollar a day.

And now, on my own front walk, I stand still with my broom and think of Eola, and I'm no longer sure it was my grandmother who taught me the proper way to sweep a sidewalk. Wouldn't it have been Eola? Not my grandmother at all but Eola, who walked down dusty roads in hand-me-down shoes to sweep my grandparents' walk every day of her working life? Wouldn't it have been Eola who offered me a turn when I asked? Eola, who let me string the beans; Eola, who traced my hand in the dough trimmings and baked me a piecrust turkey? Eola, who left behind no recipe for yeast rolls? Eola, forgotten until the seedcrowns brought her back to me on the wind?

Safe, Trapped

Inside the nest box, the baby birds are safe from hawks, sheltered from the wind, protected from the sharp eye of the crow and the terrible tongue of the red-bellied woodpecker.

Inside the nest box, the baby birds are powerless, vulnerable to the fury of the pitched summer sun, of the house sparrow's beak. Bounded on all sides by their sheltering home, they are a meal the rat snake eats at its leisure.

Things I Knew When I Was Six

LOWER ALABAMA, 1967

Flowers that bloom in the garden are called flowers, and flowers that bloom in the vacant lot are called weeds.

A grasshopper leaping away from your feet in the vacant lot sounds exactly like a rattlesnake coiled next to your feet in the vacant lot.

There is no worm hiding in the raised pink circle of skin that your grandmother calls ringworm.

From the top of a loblolly pine, your whole neighborhood looks simple and shabby and small.

When you dare your little brother to break a big rule, your brother is not the one who gets in trouble.

It's a mistake to play leapfrog with a kid who's bigger than you.

The roly-poly and the centipede both have lovely tickling feet, but the centipede will bite and the roly-poly will only roll away.

If your mother is crying and cannot stop, there's a little blue pill in the bathroom that will help her sleep.

Things I Didn't Know When I Was Six

LOWER ALABAMA, 1967

The God you believe in acts nothing like the God other people believe in.

The rhythm method is something secret for grown-ups, and it makes them very mad.

If you have a baby sister, it's because of two X chromosomes, not because you bribed your little brother to pray for the baby growing in your mother's belly to be a girl.

No black people live in your neighborhood even though black people work in every house in your neighborhood.

Just because birds eat the berries doesn't mean you can eat the berries.

Your father's new job in the city isn't better than his old job at home, but his old job went away, so the new job is lucky anyway.

Your mother wants to work too, but there are rules that don't let mothers work.

Sometimes Santa Claus has to wait till the hour before the store closes on Christmas Eve to get the markdown prices.

The hospital in Montgomery is better than the hospital at home because the hospital in Montgomery knows how to help a mother who can't stop crying.

Your mother's tears are not your fault.

Electroshock

"If the baby is a boy, he'll sleep in Billy's room," our father says. "If it's a girl, she'll sleep with you."

I pray the baby is a girl. I tell my brother I'll give him my Jell-O if he'll pray for the baby to be a girl too. When our sister is born, I hold my finger up to her hand, and she holds on, gripping tight. I cannot believe it's possible for a person to have such tiny fingers. I cannot believe such tiny fingers can grip so tightly.

"What was I like when I was a baby?" I ask our mother. "Does Lori look like me when I was a baby?"

"I don't remember very much about when you were a baby," Mama says. "That was a long time ago."

Many, many years later, she clarifies: "I don't remember much about the time just before you were born or the time after that," she says. "The treatments took all those memories away."

And now I understand: before the "treatments" gave her back her life, they took her life away.

In Mist

It came in the night on a cold wind that rattled the windows, and it lingered after the cold rains moved out this morning. It seems to mean that we will have no autumn at all this year. The long, desultory summer has finally given way, but it has not given way to fall. Winter is here now, and to signal its arrival we got just a single night of wind and rain, a single morning of mist beading in the air above the pond and blowing off with the wind.

It won't last. In Tennessee we don't get much of a winter anymore, and highs below freezing are random and uncommon. I like the idea of mist as much as I enjoy the lovely mist itself. Aren't transitions always marked by tumult and confusion? How comforting it would be to say, as a matter of unremarkable fact, "I'm wandering in the mist just now. It will blow off in a bit."

The Wolf I Love

LOWER ALABAMA, 1968

The room is quiet in that humming, vibrating way of a dark house in the country with its windows open to summer. Tree limbs brush the metal roof of the porch with a thousand discrete scratches, each branch and twig a claw. Vast, uncountable orders of insects are just beyond the screen, and every winged creature has joined the whir in the restless leaves. There's a dog sleeping under the porch, his eyes closed and his ears pricked, but I don't know he's keeping watch. My parents are upstairs in the room where I sleep when I stay here without them, and I know they will never hear me over the roar of the attic fan. They will not hear me cry out when something tears this screen away. Neither they nor my grandparents, sleeping likewise beyond my reach on the other side of the shifting house, will hear my keening when great jaws close around me and carry me into the night alone.

I am awake in a house with too many holes in it, and all that lies between me and the dark world is a rusty screen—that, and an old woman in the bed beside mine. My great-grandmother has lived to an enormous age, and I console myself by thinking of how long she has slept safely in this room, all the years she has slept with her windows open to the creaking chain of the porch swing just beyond the screen, and no harm at all has come to her in the night. I hear her sigh and turn in her bed and settle again into stillness. But when the rattle at the window starts, she is silent, and when it grows louder, she is silent still.

"Mother Ollie," I whisper. I tiptoe to her side and put my hand on her shoulder. "Mother Ollie. There's a wolf outside our window. It's trying to come in."

She reaches up and sets her soft hand on top of mine. I feel her listen. There is no sound.

"Honey, that ain't nothing but that old bird dog," she says. "Ain't no call for you to be afraid of that old bird dog."

In seconds she's asleep again, but soon enough the wolf is back, louder than before. The wolf is panting, gasping, growling. The wolf will be through that screen in an instant!

"It's back," I croak, my throat too dry for screaming. "It's back," I try again, too frightened to get out of bed to shake her.

No sooner are the words out of my mouth than the wolf draws back. No longer scuffling and grunting, it is still breathing in the darkness. I hear it breathing as my great-grandmother stirs, and then it is growling again. This time I take the two steps between our beds in a leap, tear back the sheet that covers her, and climb in. The wolf retreats.

I feel my great-grandmother shaking, and I pull the sheet up tight around us both. Her shaking erupts into chuckles. "Honey, that's just me snoring," she says, scooting over to make room for me in her narrow bed and turning on her side to reach around me and pull me closer. "Ain't no wolf gone get my girl."

BLUE JAY

Jaybird, Home

Two weeks before my seventh birthday, my family left the sandy red dirt of the wiregrass region of Lower Alabama and moved to Birmingham, a roiling city built in the shadow of Red Mountain in the southern Appalachians. The move should have been a shock—I was leaving a town untouched by open conflict for a city notorious for its racist convulsions of water cannons and police dogs and church bombings—but I was six. I knew nothing of that. I missed the pine trees.

We returned to Lower Alabama often because my grandparents still lived there, in the house where my grandfather was born, and our long family history and frequent visits might explain why I imprinted on that landscape so wholly. Or perhaps it was the open windows, a time when what happened outside the house was felt indoors, or the innocence that sent children outside to play after breakfast, not to return till hunger drove them home again. I am a creature of piney woods and folded terrain, of birdsong and running creeks and a thousand shades of green, of forgiving soil that yields with each footfall. That hot land is a part of me, as fundamental to my shaping as a family member, and I would have remembered its precise features with an ache of homesickness even if I had never seen it again.

It would take all the words in *Remembrance of Things Past* to catalog what I remember about the place where I was born, but there are three things that can bring it all back to me in startling detail: the sight of a red dirt road, the smell of pine needles, and the sound of a blue jay's call. And of those three, by far the most powerful is the call of the jaybird.

I love the blue jay's warning call, the *jeer-jeer, jeer-jeer* it makes when a hawk is near. I love the softer *wheedle wheedle wheedle* and *please please* song for its mate. Blue jays have an immense range of vocalizations—whirring and clicking and churring and whistling and whining and something you'd swear was a whisper—but the sound they make that takes me right back to 1968 is a call that mimics a squeaky screen-door hinge. I hear that sound coming from the top of a pine tree, and instantly I am in the wiregrass region of Lower Alabama, where the soil is red sand, and pine needles make a scented bower fit for all my imagined homes.

Barney Beagle Plays Baseball

It was already dark outside but not quite suppertime, late in the year we moved to Birmingham, and I don't know why I was alone with my mother in the grocery store. If my brother and sister weren't tagging along too, then my father must have been at home with them, but if Daddy was home, why did I come along with Mama to the Piggly Wiggly at the very worst time of day, when the store was swamped with husbands stopping on the way home from work to pick up the one missing item their wives needed for supper? I might never have been in the Piggly Wiggly at night before, but I knew that men did not understand the rules of the grocery store, did not understand which direction to push the cart to stay in the flow of traffic, did not recognize that standing perplexed in the middle of the aisle is bad grocery store citizenship, especially right at suppertime.

My mother was surely in a hurry. Maybe I was slowing her down as she tried to zip around the bewildered men standing despondent among the canned goods, and maybe she sent me off to pass the time in the corner of the store where books and toys were displayed. Or maybe I wandered off on my own, in those days of retail on a human scale and no thought at all that kidnappers could be lurking in the Piggly Wiggly.

The toys were a familiar, paltry offering—dusty cellophane packages of jacks and Silly Putty eggs and paddleballs and green army men—but the books were mostly new to me. The few children's books at our house belonged to an old-fashioned

era of read-aloud classics, fairy tales and nursery rhymes and
Bible stories and my own favorite, *Poems of Childhood*. The
Piggly Wiggly display featured what seemed to be a vast array
of Little Golden Books and early readers. I reached for a green
book with a picture in the foreground of a dog wearing a cap
turned sideways between its floppy ears. We didn't have a dog
ourselves. I had not yet made friends in our new city, and I
wanted a dog more than I wanted anything.

I scanned the rest of the book jacket, pausing at the picture
of boys in baseball uniforms. I had heard of baseball, but I'd
never seen a game, in person or on TV, and did not recognize
the outfits the boys were wearing. Why were these boys wearing pajamas outside on the grass? I only glanced at the words
at the top of the book jacket. I was learning in first grade the
sounds that letters make, but I could not yet read, and words
in a book meant nothing to me.

But then, as I stood in the bright light of the grocery store
with darkness pooling outside, unable to reach me, the letters
on the cover of that book suddenly untangled themselves into
words: Barney. Beagle. Plays. Base. Ball. *Barney Beagle Plays
Baseball. Oh*, I remember thinking. *Oh, it's about a dog who
plays baseball*, and opening the book to see what happened.
And only then did I realize I was actually reading the words. I
was reading! I went racing to find Mama, dodging despairing
fathers peering at can labels, to show her how I could sound
out all the words on every page and understand each one. And
she was so happy about my happiness that she told me we
could bring the book home, even though we had no money at
all, and it had not even crossed my mind that she might buy
it for me.

Creek Walk

BIRMINGHAM, 1969

The rocks are gray slate, massive slabs cantilevered over the water as though the outstretched feathers of a great prehistoric bird had been caught in stone. My brother and I are barefoot, picking our way across the rock. We are always barefoot. The pads of our feet are thick, toughened by concrete and asphalt and gravel roads, and anyway shoes would be useless on this slick rock. Worse than useless.

We have not discussed a plan, and so we are making our way to the creek bed with no real intention. We have nowhere to be and nothing to do for hours on end, for days and days on end. It is summer, and autumn is inconceivable to us. School will be reinvented every year, an astonishment every year. Where were the nuns all hiding while we were walking barefoot on the hot concrete?

We are not thinking of school or of the nuns. We are thinking of nothing, or perhaps we are wondering if we will see another rattlesnake. Seeing any snake would be a cause for remark, but we have only once seen a rattlesnake. Mainly we will turn over rocks on the bank of the creek, looking for worms and roly-polies. We aren't fishing—no one has ever taken us fishing; we are not the kind of children who would enjoy fishing—but we know we can summon fish by tossing worms into the water, and we like to feel the fish mouthing the freckles on our legs.

Sometimes there are salamanders on the bank. Sometimes there are tadpoles in the foamy water at the edges of the backwash. Sometimes there are crawdads under the rocks that jut into the water. Always there are dragonflies—blue, and bottle green, and scarlet red—hovering over the flashing water. Always there are jays scolding from the dark pines. We see them and we don't see them, we hear them and we never register their sound. The mud and the moving water smell vaguely of decay, but the smell does not disturb us or inspire the first curiosity. We have never even noted it. These are our sights and our sounds and our smells, as casual to us as the smell of our own breath in our cupped hands, as the sound of our own blood in our ears when we lie down on the biggest rock and hang our heads over the edge to dangle tickletails in the water, tricking the fish into rising.

Farther down, closer to the highway, there are words scratched into the slate on the other bank. The letters are large and ghostly white: F U C K. My brother sounds it out, a perfect practice word for someone still learning phonics from the adventures of David and Ann, the Catholic school equivalent of Dick and Jane. "Fuck," he pronounces, correctly. Then: "What does it mean?"

"It's a word people say when they're mad," I tell him.

I don't know what it means.

We pick our way back toward the bank we will climb to start heading home. Clouds of minnows race from our feet. Clouds of grasshoppers rise from the timothy grass above the rocks. Clouds of gnats hover above the water, part for our small bodies, and coalesce again behind us. We climb out and sit together on the slanted rock to wait for our feet to dry in the hot sun. At home it is almost time for supper, but we can't tell time.

Bunker

All summer long the chipmunks dart in and out of the crawl space through the tunnels they've dug under every side of our house. Open either door and a chipmunk will flee, disappearing into a potted plant, up a tree trunk, or under the front stoop where they have fashioned their bunkers. Solitary creatures except during mating season, they ignore their own kind, each keeping to its personal private entryway into the dark. They are like neighbors who check the mailbox from the car and then drive straight into the garage, never a friendly word.

In and out, the chipmunks rarely stray more than a few feet from the safety of a tunnel. There must be yards and yards of tunnels under our house by now, yards and yards and yards of tunnels, with dens tucked off to the side where the chipmunks deliver their babies in springtime, where they store their acorns in autumn, where they will sleep all winter long.

But they have not yet gone to sleep—deep into October, the temperatures remain stubbornly stuck in summer—and my husband has become unnerved by their frantic bustle as they prepare for the cold. "Look at that," he says, watching them dive for cover when he steps outside. "I think we need to take them out to the park."

"It's too late," I say. "They won't have time to get ready for winter."

"It's ninety degrees out here," he says.

He sets a catch-and-release trap outside one of the tunnels, baits it with peanut butter and birdseed, and heads to the gym. Within two minutes, there's a chipmunk in the cage, digging at the wire with its powerful rodent teeth. "Come back," I text my husband. "You caught one."

But he doesn't come back. Ten minutes pass. Fifteen. Frantically trying to chew itself to safety, the chipmunk is rubbing its gray chipmunk lips raw.

An hour later my husband regards the empty trap. "Where's the chipmunk?" he says.

"I let it go," I say.

"Oh," he says. "OK." He is the kind of man who understands that a sunny and suddenly unencumbered Sunday afternoon is a gift.

I think of the nests the chipmunks have made under our house, the chewed bits of leaves cradling blind babies with translucent skin and only the lightest down for fur. I see them though I've never seen them. I want the hawks to stay in the trees. I want my neighbors to drive carefully in the road the chipmunks keep scooting across for reasons I can't guess. I want the rat snake that lives in the brush pile to be too fat for the tunnels they have made. I want my house to shelter them.

Operation Apache Snow

When the news comes on, my father sits in his chair, swirling just one jigger of Canadian Mist in a glass of ice water and piling up ashes in a silver-rimmed coaster meant to keep the sweating glass from leaving a ring on the end table. Walter Cronkite is on the screen, and I am learning that I say everything wrong. It's ce-*ment*, not *see*-ment. And "Vietnam" is a word that rhymes with "atom bomb," not with "Birmingham." I sit on the floor, my head against my father's knee, and breathe him in: Brylcreem and Aqua Velva and cigarettes and sweat. Smoke drifts around me as Walter Cronkite gives the week's casualty count.

I look up at my brother, who is drawing a picture at the table a few feet away, his tongue tucked into the corner of his mouth, his head tilted in concentration. He has not heard a word. *He would never come home from that place*, I think. *When he leaves for Vietnam, he will not be coming back.*

Of course he will go: this war has lasted my whole life. Every week for my entire life the news report has included a count of the dead. The war will never end.

Smoke settles on my head, on my shoulders, and I practice saying "Vietnam." Viet-*nahm*. I will need to know what to say when I figure out how to get to this foreign land in my brother's place.

BLUEBIRD

Territorial

In late summer, the season of plenty gives way to the season of competition as ruby-throated hummingbirds bulk up for the coming migration, and goldfinches stuff themselves with flower seeds against a lean winter. All day long the hummingbird who has claimed my feeder tries to drive away the goldfinches, and the goldfinches try to drive away the bumblebees, and the bees try to drive away the skippers. No one tries to drive away the red wasp.

Earlier this year the cardinals lost one set of nestlings to illness and another to predators, but now at summer's end they are at the safflower feeder with two healthy fledglings. The young ones follow them around the yard, hollering, and the parents work from dawn to full night feeding them and explaining to the house finch family, over and over again, that the safflower feeder is now off-limits to everyone but juvenile cardinals. When I put mealworms out for the bluebirds, I must sit nearby while they eat, or the male cardinal—in the middle of his August molt and comically bald—will dive at them from the branches like a tiny strategic bomber. This half-acre lot belongs to him, even if the bluebirds and the house finches refuse to defer.

There is still plenty to go around—plenty of flowers, plenty of seeds, plenty of bugs—but the creatures in my yard are not interested in sharing. For them, scarcity is no different from fear of scarcity. A real threat and an imagined threat provoke the same response. I stand at the window and watch them, cataloging all the human conflicts their ferocity calls to mind.

Tell Me a Story of Deep Delight

BIRMINGHAM, 1970

We are in the double bed. I am asleep, and my sister is scooched over next to me, awake. "Tell me a story," she says loudly. She is old enough to climb out of the crib but too young to know how to whisper. "Tell me a story!"

"I'll tell you a story in the morning," I mumble.

"Tell me *one* story."

"Once upon a time there was a little girl who wanted a story, but her sister was so tired the little girl said, 'OK,' and fell asleep."

I was born for sleep. My baby sister was born for waking. "Tell me a *long* story."

"It takes a while to think of a long story," I say. "You be real quiet and let me think."

Some time later, our mother stops to check on us. The room is dark and silent, but a wedge of light from the hall falls upon her toddler's open eyes. Mama tiptoes to the edge of the bed and squats to whisper in her baby's ear. "Lori, it's late," she says. "It's so late even big girls like Margaret are sound asleep."

"Her not asleep, Mama. Her just thinking of a story."

———

As a matter of unreliable narration, this story is hard to parse. I am quoting from memory a story my mother often told, a story that came from her own memory of a time long since past. Though I have no way of knowing how accurate my mother's memory was, I'm confident that I am quoting her word for word. "Her just thinking of a story." ·

I know these words by heart because my mother told this story many times. I am less confident of my own lines, but I remember well the miniature drama that played out night after night in the old double bed that had come to us from my grandparents, and my sister remembers it too. I would pretend to be thinking of a story—or, in a version my sister swears is true though I have no recollection of it, I would tell her I had to say my prayers—and promptly go back to sleep. She would wait in the darkness, restless, impatient, until she finally fell asleep as well.

I don't know why our mother loved this story so, but my husband and I used to spy on our own young sons at night, listening to them giggling through the baby monitor, listening to them keeping each other awake in the dark. I was amazed at the way their minds worked when they had no sense of being observed—amazed at the way their lives were already unfold-ing without me. Perhaps my mother, too, loved that peek into the perfect innocence of my sister's trust. And because it was a story she told with such love and absolute delight, I think I can see it, myself:

My sister, flipping from one side to the other. Me, asleep but riding waves of consciousness with each rustle, each exas-perated sigh. Our mother, whispering to her little girl, a child full of faith, poised for a magical tale, a story made of just the right words. Waiting for them to drift over her in the darkness and lull her into dreaming.

Acorn Season

We recognize the arrival of acorn season even as the acorns still cling to the white oak growing just outside the bedroom window. They're green, but the squirrels are done with waiting. At dawn they sit in the branches of the magnificent oak and pluck the unripe nuts, taking a single bite before flinging the rejects to our roof: *BAM!* Then—*bam bam bam bam bam bam bam bam*—each one tumbles down the slope and—*BAM!*—slams into the gutter. One after another, a hailstorm of acorns, and all before the sun is up.

One morning I wake to the sound of the alarm, and I know the acorns are ripe. The squirrels are eating them now, passing over the green acorns and getting fat on the brown ones. They are all about acorns—eating them, caching them in the crooks of trees, planting them in the flower beds, in the pots on the deck, in the piles of pushed-up dirt around the mole runs. Squirrels are the Johnny Appleseeds of the oak forest, their tails bobbing up and down in an undulating arc that follows the motion of their thumbless hands, their canny fingers patting the soil gently around each acorn.

Lately the squirrels have been planting acorns in our house. Cooler nights have finally arrived, and the attic above our bedroom is the home they've chosen for winter, an alcove that can't be reached by any human. Before the alarm goes off, I lie in our room below their room and hear them running. What is the rush? They are so close I can hear them stop to scratch their fleas, but they are tucked away where I can't harm them.

They'll chew the wires and burn down your house, someone says. They carry diseases, someone says. No one says which diseases. But there is plenty of advice: poison that makes them so thirsty they'll flee, looking for water but finding instead a place to die; humane catch-and-release traps; humane traps that kill instantly. I don't want to cut a hole in my house to set a trap, and I don't want to kill them—or, worse, turn them into a slow, stumbling poison-delivery system for owls and hawks. I don't want to catch them at all. I want them to move away.

Sometimes I don't even want them to move away. I lie in bed before light and listen to the sound of their feet skittering across my ceiling, and the sound of the acorns they're rolling across it, storing food for winter. They are old friends. Their busy life above my dark room is a lullaby.

Faith

In church, under incandescent lights that make the brass candlesticks take on a golden luster, that make the polished pews gleam as though fashioned of marble, I sit between my mother and my great-grandmother, heavy bored by incense and holy water and the swishing of the priest's vestments and the clicking of his hard shoes on the hard floor. "Truly, I say to you," he intones from the ambo, "whoever says to this mountain, 'Be taken up and thrown into the sea,' and does not doubt in his heart, but believes that what he says will come to pass, it will be done for him."

I take my mother's hand and point it toward the lights. I twist it to make the light catch each facet of the diamond on fire. It is an absurd ring for someone like my mother, someone living in an apartment where the rent is paid in exchange for her trouble—for calling the plumber or the electrician whenever another tenant complains, for scheduling the grass cutters, for testing the chlorine level in the pool. The ring belonged to my father's mother, the grandmother I am named for but never met, the one my mother never met, but it has always been on her hand, and I have always played with it in church under a hundred blazing lights.

My great-grandmother's ring is not nearly so grand or so gleaming, but there is another game I play in church with Mother Ollie's hand. I take it in my own and pat it smooth, running my finger across its impossible softness, marveling at the way it ripples under my finger, as yielding as water. My great-grandmother's skin is an echo of her old Bible, the pages tissue-thin, the corners worn to soft felt. I gently pinch the skin above her middle knuckle, and then I let it go. I count to myself, checking to see how many seconds it can stand upright, like a mountain ridge made by a glacier in an age long before mine. Slowly, slowly it disappears. Slowly, slowly it throws itself into the sea.

RIVER

River Light

I try to imagine what it must have been like for the first human beings who moved through this dark forest: to glimpse a flare of light on moving water, to step out of the shadows of the close trees and see the sun flashing on a broad river. To see air and water and light conjoined in a magnificent blaze. That first instant must have felt the way waking into darkness feels—not knowing at first if your eyes are open or closed.

In that instant, the river is not a life-giving source of water and fish and passage. In that instant, it is not the roiling fury that can swallow whole any land-walking, air-breathing creature. It is only itself, unlike any other thing. It was here long before we were here, and it will be here after we are gone. It will erase all trace of us—without malice, without even recognition. And when we are gone to ground and all our structures have crumbled back to dust, the river will become again just the place where light and water and sky find each other among the trees.

Red Dirt Roads

I was eleven, my brother and our cousin ten, and we were old enough to go anywhere our legs could take us: the pecan orchard, the blackberry patch, the cemetery next to the church, the community house next to the cemetery, the store with the gas pump outside and the penny candy display just within its swinging doors. If the adults were worried about the bull a neighbor sometimes pastured among the pecan trees, or the rattlesnakes coiled under the blackberry canes, or the fire ant mounds dotting the cemetery like miniature monuments to another natural order, no one said a word to us, even though my cousin's other grandfather was killed by a rattlesnake decades before we were all born.

Surely someone gave us boundaries of some kind, marked out the territory where our wanderings had to end, but if anyone did I have no recollection of it. I don't remember whose idea it was to turn down a red dirt road between two of our grandfather's fields, a road we'd never been down before, not on foot or on the neighbor's horses. I don't remember how we decided just how far to walk before turning around and heading back to the blacktop road where our grandparents lived. Perhaps it was only the monotony of the peanuts, row after row after row. Maybe we were hot and tired, or maybe that vast, silent expanse of agriculture—uniform, blank, impersonal—began to feel alien and unwelcoming to us. We knew all the varieties of pecans by name, could gather and sort them for market unerringly, ten cents a pound, but we'd not had any hand in the peanut harvest and felt no connection to those fields.

We had already turned around, were already on the way back to our grandparents' house, when the gun appeared. That much we all agree on; that much we all remember the same way. I don't remember the feel of dust in my throat. I don't remember the red sand ringing my toenails, ground into the cuticles, though surely it must have been, for we were always barefoot—it was too hot for shoes, and sandals were useless in the actual sand. But I remember, just as my brother and my cousin remember, the sound of a truck careening down the road behind us in the silence.

Without any sense of trepidation, we moved to the side of the road to let the truck pass. I was in front, my cousin and my brother single file just behind me, though they both stepped farther off the road and drifted to my right when the truck slowed to an idle. Even before I saw the shotgun resting on the frame of the open passenger window, before I realized it was pointed straight at my head, I saw the woman's angry face peering at me from the cab. My brother and my cousin must have seen the gun first. Or perhaps they saw only the baying dogs in the bed of the truck—dogs who could have been over that tailgate in an instant.

"You got no business here," the woman said. "You got no business hanging around this road with my menfolk so close by."

I stopped walking and turned toward her. My brother or my cousin, one of them, tried to push me forward, to make me keep walking, to make me pick up speed. "This is our grand-daddy's land," I said. "We got as much business here as any-body. More than you."

"I'll not have no city girls stealing my menfolk," she said.

I laughed out loud. *Stealing her menfolk?*

Did we hear her cock the shotgun, or did we only imagine the sound? Did I stop talking then? When my brother and my cousin tell this story, they remember being afraid my back talk would get us all shot, but I don't remember a feeling of fear. I only remember thinking it was so funny, the very idea that three children—one of them a boy, though it was the 1970s, and his hair was collar length—might pose a threat to anyone old enough to drive a car or shoot a gun unsupervised.

That's what I remember: the comedy of it, the ludicrous mismatch between the visible reality of the world and some crazy grown-up's inexplicable fears.

Somehow it ended, and the woman roared off in a shower of red dirt, the dogs lurching in the truck bed before finding their footing again.

When we got home we said nothing. We only turned back to hose off our feet when Eola pointed toward the door. No one got shot. No one got bitten by a rattlesnake or gored by a bull. No harm ever came to us, though we were patently in harm's way. It was years before I understood that I was never safe, not even there.

Different

The autumnal equinox comes and goes, but you would never know it by the weather in Tennessee. Most years the temperatures remain in the nineties. The English daisies, which normally bloom in spring, come back for a second, more subdued round of greetings. My mother carried daisies in her bridal bouquet, and when they bloom I always think of her lifelong joy in their sunny faces.

One fall, a daisy sent up a bloom unlike all the others. Instead of a golden disk surrounded by an array of white petals opened mostly flat and facing toward the sun, the flower had a globe-shaped center, and the petals ringing it were perpendicular to the ground. The bees showed no preference for the ordinary daisies in my garden that year, but we humans are acutely attuned to difference and tend to prize any rare variation from the norm. We believe a four-leaf clover brings good luck. A wild crow adopts an abandoned kitten, and the video goes viral. For us, an oddly shaped daisy is cause for surprise, and then for investigation, and ultimately for delight.

With other human beings, though, we aren't so understanding. Children with any sort of physical or cognitive or emotional difference are invariably bullied, and mental illness carries such a stigma that my mother would never speak of her bouts of depression, even after I'd wrestled with depression myself.

And yet, despite our capacity for brutality, human beings are an empathetic species. In 2007, the fossil remains of a severely disabled prehistoric man were uncovered in what is now Vietnam. The skeleton revealed the fused vertebrae and weak bones characteristic of a congenital disease called Klippel-Feil syndrome. The man was a quadriplegic, unable to feed himself or keep himself clean, and yet he survived to adulthood—during the Stone Age, mind you—because others in his community took care of him.

In 1988, during one stop on our honeymoon, my husband and I visited the San Diego Museum of Man. On display at the time was an exhibit of ancient clay figures. The human figures were all visibly different in some way: people with dwarfism, people missing a limb, people with severely curved spines or extra fingers. An informational placard explained that these figures had been fashioned by members of a tribe who revered physical difference. What we call a disability they had considered a blessing: God had entrusted to the care of their community a rare treasure, and even in their art they strove to be worthy of that trust.

Be a Weed

Sometimes, when I haven't slept or the news of the world, already bad, suddenly becomes much worse, the weight of belonging here is a heaviness I can't shake. But then I think of the glister of a particular morning in springtime. I think of standing in the sunshine and watering the butterfly garden, which is mostly cultivated weeds punctuated by the uncultivated kind that come back despite my pinching and tugging. I think of the caterpillars on the milkweed plants, unperturbed by the overspray, and the resident red-tailed hawk gliding overhead, chased by a mockingbird and three angry crows, and the bluebird standing on the top of the nest box protecting his mate, who is inside laying an egg. I think of that morning—not even a morning, not even an hour—and I say to myself, *Be an egg. Be a mockingbird. Be a weed.*

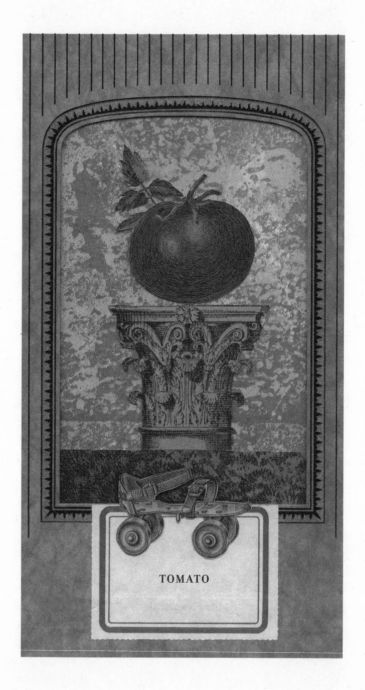

TOMATO

The Imperfect-Family Beatitudes

B lessed is the weary mother who rises before daybreak for no project or prayer book, for no reason but the solace of a sleeping house and a tepid cup of instant coffee and a fat dog curled on her lap. Hers is the fleeting kingdom of heaven.

Blessed is the suburban father whose camping gear includes two hundred yards of orange extension cord and a box fan, a pancake griddle, a weather radio, a miniature grainy-screened TV with full-sized rabbit ears, and another box fan. He shall keep peace in the menopausal marriage.

Blessed is the farm-born mother, gripped by a longing for homegrown tomatoes, who nails old roller skates to the bottom of a wooden pallet, installs barrels of soil and seeds on top, and twice a day tows it through the grass to the bright spots, following slivers of sun across the shady yard. She shall taste God.

Blessed is the fatherless father who surrenders his Saturdays to papier-mâché models of the Saturn V rocket or sugar-cube igloos or Popsicle-stick replicas of Fort Ticonderoga, and always to scale. In comforting he shall be comforted.

Blessed is the mother whose laugh is a carillon, a choir, an intoxication filling every room in the house and every dollar-movie theater and every school-play performance, even when no one else gets the joke. She will be called a child of God.

Blessed is the winking father who each day delivers his children to Catholic school with a kiss and the same advice: "Give 'em hell!" He will be summoned to few teacher conferences.

Blessed is the braless mother who arrives at the school pickup line wearing pink plastic curlers and stained house shoes, and who won't hesitate to get out of the car if she must. She will never be kept waiting.

Blessed are the parents whose final words on leaving—the house, the car, the least consequential phone call—are always "I love you." They will leave behind children who are lost and still found, broken and, somehow, still whole.

Night Walk

It's a crazy cartoon of a moon, over the top even by Hollywood standards. No one would ever believe this moon on a movie screen: the outrageous roundness of it, the deep gold hue, the way it's settled in the center of a soft nest of light against a warm black sky, above stark black branches. Gray clouds are rushing across it in a wind so high the moon winks and recovers as quickly as it would in a time-lapse film.

What a rebuke this weather has been to my own frequent claims that fall and spring are the seasons of change, that nothing much happens in winter. The last days have brought balmy, shirtsleeves sun and brutal, bone-tightening cold and this tree-bending wind. And now the wind is bearing in a cold rain, already sputtering down in horizontal pellets.

When the moon no longer emerges from the clouds and the rain picks up, the dark world closes. The screen goes black, and now the soundtrack is all that matters. A neighbor's wind chimes jangle, and then another's. A clatter of bare sycamore branches and a lighter rattle of seedpods in the dried trumpet vines climbing a power pole. The snapping fabric of a flag. A castanet of stiff leaves in an ancient magnolia standing unperturbed in the rush of air. Maple leaves scudding down the rough asphalt. A train whistle. A siren. A wary greeting from the three-legged dog behind her fence, warning me to come no closer in the dark.

Every Time We Say Goodbye

"Every time we say goodbye, I die a little," Ella Fitzgerald is singing while my parents dance on an ordinary Tuesday afternoon. My mother is barefoot. My father is wearing his work shoes, but my mother's toes are in no danger. These steps are as familiar to them as their own heartbeats. As familiar as the words of this song.

I stand in the doorway and watch, embarrassed by something I can't even name. My father's arm is around my mother's waist. My mother is on tiptoe, her arm across his shoulders, her head tucked beneath his cheekbone. Their other hands are intertwined, held between their hearts. Their steps are so practiced, so perfectly in sync, not a single inch opens between them as they spin.

Gall

At a dinner party, I ran into another writer whose subject is often backyard nature—a writer who lives in the same town, though we'd never met in real life before. "So you're a trained naturalist?" she asked. I had to confess I'm more of a Googler. I grew up playing in the woods, and all my life I've turned to woodland paths when the world is too much with me, but I am no scientist. It took a lot of nerve for someone so ignorant of true wilderness to fashion herself as a nature writer, but the flip side of ignorance is astonishment, and I am good at astonishment.

One spring I was standing at our bedroom window with my camera, using the zoom lens to search for a house wren I could hear but couldn't see, when I noticed something odd on a branch of the oak tree that grows just outside the window. A spongy white pod, about the size of a golf ball, protruded from the very tip of a thin branch. I had never seen one before and couldn't guess what it was. A cancerous growth? A cocoon? The seedpod of a parasitic plant? And what search-engine terms could possibly yield an answer?

"Puffy white ball on the end of an oak twig" finally turned up an image that matched the object on my own oak tree. It was a growth called a gall. There are many different kinds of galls, but this one was made by the wool sower gall wasp, a small black insect that lays its eggs in winter at the tender ends of young branches. The eggs hatch in springtime, just as the twig begins to put on new growth. Then the larvae produce a chemical secretion that forces the tree to form a gall, a protective woolly home where they can live until they are ready to take to the air.

The transformation of any sort of grub into any sort of winged being is a metamorphosis I will rearrange my life to witness, so I checked on the woolly gall every day, many times a day, hoping to be on hand the precise moment the young wasps emerged into the light of springtime.

The oak, meanwhile, was not ready to surrender its own purposes: instead of wool sower gall wasps, what emerged from the gall was a pair of perfectly formed but apparently dwarfed leaves. In time these leaves began to stretch out languidly, not exactly like but also not entirely unlike a typical oak leaf. The gall was taking on the appearance of something pregnant with an alien life-form, and that alien fully intended to hatch.

More than a month passed with no sign of the wasps. I continued to peer at the gall through my bedroom window, if less and less often throughout the day. By the time another month passed, the gall had begun to shrivel and collapse in on itself. Clearly, I had missed the emergence of the wasps, but I kept going to the window to look at the gall anyway, out of a vague remaining curiosity, and possibly out of habit, too.

What I wanted, I think, was some sort of closure, some reckoning of what it means when a thing in nature makes what it needs from only what it has on hand. But as with all other matters in nature and in life, I entered this story in medias res: unaware of its beginning and owed no right to witness its end.

The Honeymoon

The day I started my first period, my father invited me for a walk after supper. It was a typical walk, a familiar habit, until he spoke: "Your mother tells me you became a woman today," he said.

He was holding my hand—at thirteen I was still holding my father's hand with half my body even as I was bleeding with the other half—and reflexively I pulled away. Are there any words more appalling to a girl savoring the privacy of new transformation? If a volcano had erupted below my feet in the heart of Alabama, I would gladly have gone up in ash.

My mother had offered nothing beyond the pragmatics: instructions on how to work the straps to the belt that came with the box of pads she'd pulled down from her closet shelf. How often to change the pad. How to wrap it up and take it to the kitchen trash can, which the family dachshund could not reach. The absolute, unvarying importance of that trash can.

I never knew if she had asked my father to broach the subject, or if she had merely passed along the day's news over the glass of whiskey they always shared before supper, a relic of postwar civility in the chaotic days of Watergate and Vietnam and never enough money in our hollow-doored apartment outside town.

Catholics aren't squeamish about sexuality, and my education at Our Lady of Sorrows School had already included a unit on human reproduction, including a poster-sized diagram of the female reproductive system and a teacher armed with a pointer stick and a holler-it-out insistence on correct pronunci-ation: fa-*loh*-pee-an, *oh*-va-ry, en-do-*mee*-tree-um, *clit*-or-is. All in the context of a religion-class unit on family life and the moral implications of sexuality.

It would take more than a year for Mom to make her own half-hearted attempt at The Talk. I laughed out loud before she'd gotten a whole sentence out of her mouth, and that was the end of the subject. In all the years afterward, I never heard her make even a veiled reference to her own sexual life or to mine. My mother, I decided, was something of a prude.

I don't remember when I found the lone honeymoon photo in my father's sock drawer. It was a black-and-white Polaroid of Mom wearing a frothy gown-and-peignoir set. She's stand-ing in a doorway, her hair freshly brushed, and the corner of a bed is visible in the foreground. Her smile is open, utterly guileless, happy.

"Where's this?"

"I took it on our wedding night," my father said, taking the photo from me and peering at it. It was a picture of Mom moments before she joined him in bed for the first time—a pic-ture of a woman who was not suffering even a hint of shyness.

As a child I would ask my mother, "But why did you wait so long to get married?"

Sometimes she would cite, obliquely, the Catholic prohi-bition against birth control: "We couldn't afford to have a fam-ily yet." Sometimes she would say, "We loved to dance. Once we got married and the babies came along, there wouldn't be many chances to go dancing."

No money for children. No money for a sitter. *I* was the reason they had waited so long. I, who lived nestled in their love like a world-sized cradle. I, who had always felt so sub-limely like the center of their universe. They hadn't wanted me to join them yet. They had wanted to keep dancing.

After my mother's death, I found the rest of the honeymoon pictures in a box that had sat in an Alabama attic for more than fifty years. In the one I think of as the morning-after companion to the wedding-night picture, Mom is the photographer, and Dad is the subject, standing before the mirror in a motel bathroom, shaving. But it's Mom I like to imagine. I think I can see her, barefoot in the doorway to the bedroom, relishing the intimacy of life with her new husband, the man who had not yet become my father.

In Which My Grandmother Tells the Story

of Her Brother's Death

LOWER ALABAMA, 1976

I've left out when Wilfred died, haven't I? Well, in May—no, in June—of 1976, he was down to go with us to the church reunion, and he had Joseph with him, his first grandchild, and was so proud of him. And Mother went home with them that Sunday, to be there with them the next Sunday, which would be Father's Day. Wilfred left for a business trip on Tuesday. And of course he kissed them goodbye, and on Thursday they called to say they had found him dead in a motel room where he had gone back to take some medicine, some blood pressure medicine. Well, it upset us terribly because we had just seen him so well.

Mother, of course, was brokenhearted because she had lost a child. When she went to the casket to see him the first time, she stood there and looked at him and said, "Why couldn't it have been me?" And she sobbed, and that's the only time she cried. When they brought her to our house on the day of the funeral, I went out and hugged her. And she had a few little tears but not much. She was real composed. And so he was buried on Saturday before the Father's Day that she was to spend with him.

Squirrel-Proof Finch Feeder,

Lifetime Warranty

The steel grommets around the miniature openings, fit only for conical beaks, cannot be chewed open by even the most persistent rodent. Both the top and the bottom of the feeder detach for ease in filling and cleaning, but the pegged fittings can't be managed by thumbless hands. The seed is black niger—a feast for goldfinches, distasteful to squirrels. So say the experts at the bird supply store.

The experts have not met this squirrel. He takes the feeder by the perches, one in each hand, pulling it to his mouth like an ear of sweet corn at a Fourth of July potluck. He makes his own mouth small to match the cleft mouth of the feeder, and he licks the seeds out, one by one. This is an embrace, a kiss that goes on for hours. Seed by seed, he fills his belly. He has nothing but time, and the squirrel-proof finch feeder, impervious to fury and force, is undone by patience and time. He knows I am at my desk barely more than an arm's reach from the window, but I do not concern him. I am only watching through the window, and I do not in any way concern him.

There Always Must Be Children

At the end of our great-uncle's funeral, our great-aunt stopped the pallbearers as they carried him out of church. She fell upon the casket, trying to reach with her frail arms all the way around it and wailing like one whose own life was ending. All five of us, my brother and sister and both cousins, watched from the front pew, entirely untouched by devastating loss. Our parents and grandparents went to our aunt and surrounded her and held her up when her legs could no longer bear her weight.

We looked at each other. What would happen next? And what would we ourselves be called upon to do? Our favorite aunt, howling with uncontainable grief, resembled no human being we had ever seen.

When the next-youngest child coughed to disguise a laugh, the rest of us collapsed between the pews. We huddled together on the board floor and buried our faces in our arms, strangled by swallowed laughter.

Tracks

Walking around the neighborhood soon after we moved
to the house that decades later he would die in, my father tapped his toe against the place on the side of the road
where rusted trolley-car tracks emerged from the asphalt.
"Every day I would wait right here for my father to get home
from work," he said. "Every day he got off the trolley and
asked, 'Have you been a good boy?' And every day I would
have to tell him no." He hadn't minded his mother, or he'd
fought with his brother, or he'd bothered the chickens. And
then the grandfather I never met would walk home with the
little boy who grew up to be my perfect father, and he would
spank that child with a belt.

My grandfather died in a car accident when my father was
five years old, and my father remembered almost nothing
about him except one thing: that every day when he was a boy
he would meet his father at the trolley stop and walk home
with him for a beating.

In Which My Grandmother Tells the Story

of My Grandfather's Death

LOWER ALABAMA, 1977

L*et me see, it was on the Thursday before Christmas. I brought him home from the hospital, and he seemed so happy, and I was happy. I'd had him a chair moved in—I bought a chair and had them to bring it. I said, "Be sure to have it there by ten o'clock," so they had. The hospital had one that he could sit in and press himself up. He had said, "I want a chair like this," just offhandedly, so that was the kind it was.*

In the car I could see him observing the trees and where things had been planted and just everything. He was very alert. And we drove into the yard, and Max Junior was there under the pecan tree. So we got Max out with his walker, and he walked around the front of the car, and we got the door open, and he got just inside the door. And I said, "You see your Christmas gift over there?" and he nodded his head.

And that was it. His feet began slipping out, and I held him until he got to the floor, and Max Junior and I did all we could. Neither one of us knew much about resuscitation. And Nina called down to the store, and there wasn't but one man there and he came, but she also called the paramedics. And everybody worked on him. I don't think he ever breathed again.

We got to the hospital, and the doctor came out and said, "It was just too late."

"No," I said. "Is he gone?"

And he said, "Yes. It was just too late."

Well, Max Junior and I both just almost collapsed. The doctor got hold of us and he said, "If I had been right there I couldn't have done anything." Said, "Everything about him just quit at once."

And we went back and called Olivia, and of course all of you were there by morning. Now that was on Friday, you see. Well, we had to bury him on Christmas Eve. And the day of his funeral it was just pouring rain, and I remember very distinctly how many people came anyhow, even if it was Christmas Eve and raining like it was.

And when we got back to the house I went to bed, and all five of y'all came in there quietly—I wasn't asleep, but you came in there very quietly—and said, "Mimi, will it be all right for us to fix a Christmas tree?" I said, "Sure you can." I said, "Granddaddy would want you to."

MARIGOLD

My Mother Pulls Weeds

The kitchen can be full of unwashed dishes, both counters covered in granules of spilled sugar and puddles of congealed milk. The tops of the curtains can be dusted with droppings from the cockatiel who screeches his sorrow so plaintively that she cannot bear to cage him for long. The chairs in the living room can be piled high with laundry, and magazines dated years earlier, and junk mail still leaved together with the unpaid bills, and my sister's forgotten schoolwork, the manifold worksheets of a child still in elementary school. My mother's need for order has nothing to do with the chaos of a life with too little space and too little money and almost no chance to make something beautiful of it all. The chance to create loveliness is always waiting just past the door of our matchbox rental.

She never prepares for gardening—no special gloves, no rubber garden clogs, no stiff canvas apron with pockets for tools. No tools, most of the time. She steps out of the house—or the car, setting her bags down before she even makes it to the door—and puts her hands in the soil, tugging out the green things that don't belong among the green things that do. Now another bare square of ground appears, and there is room for marigold seeds, the ones she saved when last year's ruffled yellow blooms turned brown and dried to fragile likenesses of themselves. The light bill might be under the covers at the foot of her bed, the unsigned report card somewhere in the mess of papers on the mantel, but she can always put her hands on last year's seeds. And later, in the summer, the very ground she walks on will be covered in gold.

Fly Away

His face was ridiculous: the rouged cheeks of Raggedy Andy, an elaborate Kabuki crest. He had the run of the house, swooping from curtain rod to curtain rod and door top to door top, joyfully shredding the newspaper and nibbling the spines of my books, his round gray tongue probing at the bindings, searching for glue. Though he knew a few human words, he spoke mostly in his own inscrutable language, muttering conspiracies to my sister's toys, shuffling among the stuffed animals and attempting to incite a riot. Claiming a teddy bear for his mate, he hissed at my sister, his yellow crest flattened, if she tried to take it away.

When I called, he flew to me, but he bit my lip at least as often as he held still for a kiss. He loved to be scratched, offering up each angle of his face to my fingers, and his trust thrilled me. I rubbed behind his crest, under his white-ringed eyes, beneath his gray beak. I could feel the hot skin beneath his feathers and the swift pulse just beneath the skin. When new feathers came in, he would present himself for preening, waiting as I unfurled each one, rolling them between my fingers. The powdery new feathers smelled earthy and alien at once.

He came to harm at times—singed feathers when he flew too close to an open flame on the gas range, an entire toenail lost to a slammed door—but he complained so bitterly in his cage, pacing the wooden perch, biting the bars, clutching the closed door with both feet and screeching, that we always gave in to his demand for freedom. The bounded freedom of our 1,300-square-foot house.

Inevitably, he flew away. Propping the storm door open with her hip one day, my mother stooped to pick up a bag of groceries, and he landed on her head before launching himself into the sky. He lingered in a tall pine, waddling along one branch and hopping to another as I stood below, holding my finger in the air and calling. Soon I couldn't see him in the gathering gloom, but I followed the sound of his voice as he talked to himself: "Pretty bird. Kiss, kiss, kiss." I didn't see him leave the pine.

Days later, more than a week, a miracle: my father woke me on Sunday morning, newspaper in hand. There, in full color, perched on an old man's finger, was our wayward cockatiel. We knew him instantly by the missing nail on his crooked gray toe. My father called the paper and somehow reached the photographer, who gave vague directions and a general description of the house.

We made the drive past factories and industrial parks to a part of town that couldn't rightly be called "town" anymore, with dirt driveways, bunched trailers and clapboard shacks, and lots overgrown with struggling saplings. A world I couldn't reconcile with the world.

We knew the house by the broken-down car out front, a cinder block where one of its wheels should have been, and the peeling red paint. It was some time before the old man from the photograph answered our knock. Opening the door, he stepped back, and my father stepped back too, explaining. The man pointed at the car. "No window screens here at the house," he explained.

I took the steps two at a time. The bird was lying on the back seat, his feet curled, his body still warm—from the heat of the closed car, perhaps, or because he'd died even as we stood on that porch asking for him. I held him in my hands and wept, pressing him to my face. All I remember for sure of that moment is his familiar smell. And the sight of my father and the old man standing together, side by side, at the bottom of the crumbling steps.

Church of Christ

One day my father picked me up from the children's shoe store where I worked after school and pulled into the Church of Christ parking lot around the corner from our house. Then he shut off the car and said, "Your mother's been crying all day. She thinks you don't love her."

I looked at him. I had no idea what he was talking about. "Why would she even *think* that?"

"She says you had an argument this morning. She wouldn't tell me what it was about or what you said to her. What could you have possibly said to your mother to make her cry all day?"

I was seventeen. I had given no thought to my mother that day. I gave hardly any thought to either of them on any day at all. Even prompted in the dark church parking lot, I could not recall a single conversation that might have made my mother cry.

I said, "I don't remember having a fight with Mom before school."

Migrants

Every spring my bird-watching neighbor across the street tells me she is waiting for the rose-breasted grosbeaks to return to her feeders for a day or two during their long, long migration, and every spring they turn up, right on time, to feast on the safflower seeds she puts out especially for them. I keep a safflower feeder up all the time—primarily to discourage visits from European starlings, who dislike safflower seeds—and so I started looking for the rose-breasted grosbeaks every spring, too. I was always disappointed.

Then, one year, I had grosbeaks every day for two solid weeks. At first they were skittish, heading into the trees as soon as I stepped out the door, but they got to know me. I could walk around the deck, watering plants, sweeping, and they would peer at me from the back side of the feeder for a few moments before going back to their meal. All day long they lined up for a turn, it seemed, waiting on the nearest branches until a perch opened up at the feeder.

Tennessee is just a way station for the grosbeaks, who spend winter deep in the rain forests of Central and South America but mate and rear their young primarily in the northernmost reaches of the United States and Canada. Appalachia appeals to them too, and my neighbor is sure that our guests are headed to the mountains of northern Georgia. And why not? Her guess seems as good as any.

But guessing is getting harder to do as the songbird migration is complicated by the effects of climate change. The timing of spring has shifted, and migratory songbirds, leaving the equatorial jungles at the usual time, arrive in North America too late for the food sources they expect to encounter along the way. For thousands and thousands of years, the path of the migrating songbird has been synced to the growing season of plants that now bloom and fade out of their once typical seasons. What will the birds eat if the berries they rely on have long since withered by the time they arrive? Is that why the grosbeaks—one of the species most affected by changing climate patterns—finally came to my feeder? Why they came and stayed and stayed and stayed?

Wherever they have been, and wherever they are going, it's the birds only passing through our region that excite the most interest from serious birders. I am not myself a serious birder, but I still feel a thrill when I notice a new face at the feeder, a stranger at the birdbath. I treasure these glimpses of the exotic, this sense of having traveled to distant lands, and hearing, however briefly, their strange, foreign songs. One evening I looked out, and there in the growing twilight was a male scarlet tanager taking a drink. I had never seen one in this yard before, and I have not seen one since. But I think often of that beautiful bird, of the few seconds I could stand at my window and watch him taking drink of water in the gloaming. To me he looked like a blood-red, hollow-boned embodiment of grace.

Prairie Lights

Even in a land-yacht station wagon, we were piled in too tight: in the back seat, my high school boyfriend and his angry sister, with me between them so their skin never touched in the heat; their parents up front; the little brothers ricocheting around in the wayback with all the suitcases. When we were halfway across the endless Midwest, moving fifty-five miles an hour through towering forests of corn and sunflowers, the car's anemic air-conditioning went out entirely and with it any cheer that could be produced by an I Spy game or a lunchroom carton of chocolate milk from the cooler on the front seat.

When we got to the tidy town on the plains of Colorado, all the aunts and uncles and cousins poured out of the grandmother's house, a great constellation of kindness come to meet us and welcome the family home. Someone mentioned that the Perseids would be putting on a fine display the following night, and someone else offered to bring blankets to the clan's usual spot on the prairie, and my boyfriend's father explained that I, a child of the damp, congealed air of Alabama, had never seen a night full of stars like the one I would see that night in the high, thin air above the plains of Colorado.

Though it was August, we had to put on sweaters when they woke us deep in the night, and though we were all still so tired from two days of driving in the heat, my boyfriend and his sister didn't quarrel, laughing instead to remember another childhood trip to see another meteor shower, and when we turned off the road onto the grass, the soil of the prairie was not at all flat and smooth but jarred us till our heads bumped the roof of the station wagon. Everything surprised me. I understood that I understood nothing at all.

And, oh, the stars were like the stars in a fairy tale, a profligate pouring of stars that reached across the sky from the edge of the world to the edge of the world to the edge of the world. Even before the first meteor winked at the corner of my eye, I tilted my head back and felt the whole planet spinning, and instantly I dropped to the ground and hunted for something to hold fast to before the prairie tilted and tossed me into the black void that holds this tiny blue world.

In silence the family lay together, quilts set edge to edge. Across the grass I could hear the mother still trying to coax one of the younger boys out of the car, telling him she would hold him tight, but he would not budge. "I'm too little," he said. "It's too big, and I'm too little."

ECLIPSE

A Ring of Fire

In the winter of 1991, my brother read Annie Dillard's ec-static essay about watching a total eclipse, decided then and there to see it for himself, and looked up his next chance to see one in the continental United States. When that date turned out to be impossibly far in the future—not till 2017—he and my sister-in-law made plans to view another eclipse from a mountain in rural Mexico, the nearest possible place to see the shadow of the moon obscure the sun.

There is some disagreement now about what they actually saw. My sister-in-law remembers a wall of darkness hurtling toward her across the Mexican valley, just as Annie Dillard describes. My brother only remembers reading about it. Did they see the shadow of the moon traveling across the land at 1,800 miles an hour, or did they conflate the experience of reading about an eclipse with actually seeing one? Could it have happened so fast that an ill-timed blink meant my brother missed what my sister-in-law saw?

I wanted to see this exceedingly rare phenomenon too, but I didn't want to see it in some distant, unfamiliar part of the world. I wanted to see it in my own country, in the company of blue jays. I wanted to see splintered light glinting on all the intricate webs that our own microthena spiders had strung across narrow footpaths in the night. I wanted to see sun par-ings wink through the wild rose of Sharon flowers—an effect of the partial eclipse that turns a forest into a great pinhole camera, projecting images of the waning sun onto the ground and leaving moon-shaped holes in all the shadows.

In 2017, I had my chance. I arrived at a nearby field in a

public park to find it already ringed by people speculating about exactly when each known effect would take place. When would the color of the sky deepen? When would the air begin to shimmer, as though lighted by some other planet's sun? When would the birds fly into the trees to roost?

Then there was my own unvoiced question: When it's all over, will I know what I saw? Will I be able to tell the difference between what I saw and what I had merely been primed to see?

I still don't know. I know only that something ineffable, something beyond the reach of my own language, happened in the ordinary sky. The air turned blue and then silver. A dog barked. A bird whose song I don't know began to sing and then abruptly fell silent. The air cooled, and suddenly Venus was gleaming in the midnight-blue pitch of the sky. The people under the trees at the edges of the meadow had moved into the darkness of the open field. By the time I looked down again, they had gathered a sheen that made them all look like angels.

And at the center of everything was a ring of fire in the sky, a thin sliver of flame that burned as brightly as the sun but was nothing like the sun. It was nothing like anything else I have ever seen, but I recognized it anyway because it was exactly like something I have heard. In Nashville, you can hear it wafting from the open door of any honky-tonk: a song about love, about desire. Like desire, it burned, burned, burned, and it made me feel puny and insignificant but also ablaze with life. The ancients believed an eclipse would bring the end of the world, but the end of the world did not come for me.

I didn't wait for the sun to wax full again before heading home. I had to get out of there without talking to any of my fellow mortals, without hearing any of their earthly concerns. I had to leave while the air was still full silver. And all the way home, tiny crescents bespeckled the road, a path of fractured light that led me back to my own place in the world, right to my very door.

Once Again, the Brandenburgs

By the spring of our senior year, we knew our teacher was dying. In truth she had been dying for some time, since the winter we were juniors, but her faith was unshakable, and she had young children at home, and so she believed this cancer, like the one that had claimed her breasts when she was only a teenager, was just a blackberry winter—an out-of-season cold snap that will not last or cause permanent damage. We believed, too, because how could we not? We were children. Death had no hold on us.

Spring came to Alabama, but it did not come to our teacher, whose hair was gone by then, her voice barely more than a whisper. She had long since ceased to lead the class in any conventional way. On good days a family member would drive her to school and help her to our classroom, but most days were not good by then, and she would send someone from home to collect our work or give us another task. Assignments came through her wavering voice played back on a cassette tape—notes on what to look for in our reading, assignments for our presentations on Shakespearean tragedy or the Romantic poets or the novels of Thomas Hardy. I remember so much about those books and plays and poems, the kinds of details I remember from no other high school class. I still know great chunks of *King Lear* by heart.

Of all the memorable moments of that memorable year, the one that has held me through my own calamities is a story we read the spring we realized our teacher was dying. She came into class carrying a thin box of records and a sheaf of photo-copied papers, and behind her came her stepfather, pushing a cart from the library that held a record player.

But here the recollection comes undone. Picturing that day now, I'm suddenly not sure about those papers I think I see stacked on top of the box of records in her arms. Maybe she didn't hand out the story as copies; maybe it was bound instead in the textbook we had hardly opened all year. All these images are absolutely clear, but I know better than to trust them. I have turned them over so often the edges have become soft and worn, their contours wholly unreliable.

I know it was the story of a man during wartime who sat in the back of a boxcar and closed his eyes and removed himself from the massacre by playing Bach's Brandenburg Concertos in his mind. And after we had read it, our teacher opened the top of the record player, carefully removed an LP from its sleeve, and placed it on the turntable. When she set the needle down, the sound of Brandenburg Concerto no. 1 filled that windowless, cinder-block room.

I could not believe that something so beautiful, so other-worldly, had been conceived by a human mind and brought to life by human hands. So many of the other details of that day have fallen away—surely there was a class discussion, though I don't recall it—but that high, haunting violin in the second movement of Bach's Brandenburg Concerto no. 1 in F Major is something I will remember till I die.

It has been decades since the English class that burned itself into me and the death of the teacher whom I will always love. As grief has piled on grief in that way of time, I think I've come to understand why a soldier would find solace in such timeless music, which I have heard since then in recordings and on the radio more times than I can count. But when I heard it live for the first time, when I sat and listened to an orchestra play all six Brandenburg concertos, all I could think of, in the midst of that unfathomable beauty, was a line from *Lear.* "Why should a dog, a horse, a rat, have life, / And thou no breath at all?"

While I Slept

I was dreaming about babies in cages, and while I slept it be-gan to snow. Piled deep, hushed and hushing, it rounded the rough edges of the world in a way I'd seen before only in picture books and movies. I came downstairs in the unfamiliar house to peer from the windows in the kitchen. In the stillness before dawn the room seemed full of light, though all I could see outside were shades of sepia and iron, ocher and ash. The gray was muffled, giving way to whiteness.

I was visiting a friend at his childhood home, a prewar infir-mary on the grounds of an orphanage. The tour he'd given me only hours before already seemed like a dream summoned by the bewilderment of travel. But it was not a dream. Abandoned children still lived in the dormitory buildings just across the way. My friend's father ran the orphanage, and the infirmary had been refitted for him and his family. Their bedrooms were in the old nurses' quarters on ground level. The ancient clinics were below in the basement. The operating room—its instru-ment trays and enamel tables left behind, thick with dust—was on the second floor, where I was sleeping. Most forsaken of all was the dormered attic that once served as a nursery: metal cribs still lined the walls.

I stood at the window in the dim kitchen and watched the snow pour from the sky. I don't know how long I stood there before something just outside the window began to take shape in the dawn light, something alive with movement and still somehow immobile. Finally a bird feeder untangled itself from the limb of a hackberry tree, and all around it cardinals were jostling for space. The snow was falling, and they were falling too, and rising again—a blur of movement within movement against the still backdrop of fallen snow and black branches, a scarlet tumult reeling from feeder to spilled seed and back, again and again and again. I stood in the window and watched. I watched until I knew I could keep them with me, until I believed I would dream that night of wings.

PIEBALD FAWN

Seeing

I have poor vision, the result of an uncorrected lazy eye. In some babies born with amblyopia, the lazy eye wanders, but my eyes had no noticeable misalignment, so no one knew I was seeing with only one eye. The way to improve a lazy eye is to patch the dominant eye, but the window for correction is small. By the time I finally went to an ophthalmologist, I was nearly thirty years old—decades past the age when a patch would do any good.

Because the part of the brain that develops in conjunction with the eyes did not receive sufficient input during those early years, I still see mainly through one eye and always imperfectly, even with glasses. I was born into a strong family history of blindness—my grandmother went blind from glaucoma, my mother had macular degeneration, her brother suffered blood clots in both eyes—and I take no day with vision for granted. I am filled with gratitude for the sight I have.

And yet I can't help but wish I could see better. I look forward every spring and fall to the songbird migration, but I have only rarely seen the tiny traveling wrens and warblers. Binoculars are of limited help when the brain doesn't develop in a way that produces binocular vision—although if someone says to me, "Look!" and points in the right direction, binoculars can give me a good idea of what's there. To see the smallest creatures truly, I rely on a camera with a zoom lens, and even then I have to upload the images to my computer and look at them on a larger screen to know for sure what I've photographed.

One of the nicest things about the lake where I like to walk is that there is nearly always someone on the trail saying, "Look!"

Thanks to that natural human urge to share something wonderful, even with a stranger, I have learned this lake's terrain over the years and know where to look for the well-disguised secrets I would miss on an unfamiliar path. I know that a barred owl frequently perches in a dead tree near a particular bridge. I know that a great blue heron often stands as still as a photograph on a submerged log in one cove. I know the rise where wild turkeys drag their wing feathers on the ground and blend in with the leaf litter, and I know the bank where beavers climb soundlessly out of the lake. One summer I knew where to look for a hidden hummingbird's nest because of a stranger with better eyes than mine.

I also knew where to look for a piebald fawn who was born in these woods late one spring, but knowing where to look is not the same thing as seeing what you're looking for. Walking around the lake with my niece that fall, I mentioned that I'd long been hoping to see the white fawn, and half a minute later she said, "Look! There it is!" And there the fawn surely was, coming through the trees, her mother and twin right beside her.

That fawn was a sight to behold, glowing among the shadows, picking her way through the white snakeroot grown nearly as tall as she was. At one spot, following her mother, she seemed to encounter an obstacle too large to step over and took a sudden leap into the air. For an instant her delicate hooves flashed in the late afternoon light. If I'd had a camera, and if I'd clicked the shutter at just that moment, she would have looked as though she were taking flight.

The trail was busy—the trail is always busy on weekend afternoons in pretty weather—and all around us people were saying to each other, "Look!" and stopping to watch the piebald fawn walking along the deer path. Parents were picking up their children and holding them high: "Look!"

Farther down the trail, my beautiful niece, whose eyes see twenty-twenty even without glasses, paused before a fallen tree covered with shelf fungi. She pointed to a ladybug nearly hidden in the folds. "When I was hiking in Colorado, I saw a whole bunch of ladybugs, so I checked Google to see if there's a name for a group that gathers in one place," she said. "It's called a 'loveliness.'"

In Which My Grandmother Tells the Story

of Her Mother's Death

LOWER ALABAMA, 1982

Well, *sometime after that, then, Mother broke her hip. After we got her out of the hospital, we thought we were going to bathe her, but she wouldn't let us bathe her. There's a place in the Bible that says the children should not look on their parents uncovered, or something like that. I don't remember the words, but she was a firm believer of that. She'd let Eola bathe her, though.*

She continued walking with her walker, but was having terrible pain. She was real touchy on her hip. And so we went back to the doctor, and he made X-rays. And he said, "The pins have slipped." Said, "They're going into the flesh is the reason you're having so much pain." And said, "Now, I can take them out right here in the office and give you relief, but you won't ever walk anymore." But said, "We can go to surgery, and I can put in a ball." And so she said that's what she wanted to do.

The surgery went great, and it don't seem like it was very many days before they began taking her to therapy. And she came in one time, and she was just smiling. And she says, "I took a few steps today." And so we were all just so pleased.

But she didn't want to eat, and I was trying to get her to eat. And I said, "Oh, Mother, don't do like that!" when I was trying to feed her. And she looked at me, you know, so strange, and she said, "You don't usually talk to me like that." I was scolding her.

The next morning, I reckon it was, I was in the room with her, and I got up and walked over to Mother and put my hands on her arm, and it was just burning up. So about that time the doctor walked in, and I said, "Doctor, she is just burning up with fever." He switched right around and went to the desk, and he called the other doctor, and they got me out of the room and they did a spinal tap, and she was all the time saying, "Mildred, don't let them do this." And you know I couldn't do anything about it, and Mother never did talk anymore after that.

When Olivia called that time, she said, "Mother, you want me to come?"

And I said, "Well, why don't you wait until we go home."

And she said, "I'm coming for you, not for Mother Ollie."

The next morning they said, "She's become a medical problem now," and they moved us up to the next floor. I always will feel angry toward them. Because they knew she was dying.

They got her in this room, and she laid just as quiet, didn't move a muscle. I had gotten my cot in, and Olivia was sitting in the big chair, and she was where she could see Mother Ollie, you know. And finally she said, "Mother Ollie's not breathing." And she was gone just like that.

Redbird, Sundown

Everywhere else, in every other place where the wide sky reaches, the space beyond the trees is still blue, the black branches spread out on a flat plane as if cut from construction paper, as if pasted in delicate tracery on an azure scrim. The pure, blinding blue that reaches from treetop to treetop in the east is the only sign that this is not a sepia world made entirely of brown grass and rustling beech leaves, pale as dawn light, and the dormant hydrangea's dry ghost petals and the white scaling of the sycamore.

The earth has faded, but the sky will not give up its right to color, doubling down in the west with reds and oranges and yellows. The light catches in the bare branches of the maple and clothes it in a fleeting dream of autumn, all pink and auburn and gold. The cardinal perched near the top of the tree bursts into radiance, into flame, and for that moment nothing matters at all—not the still soil nor the clattering branches nor the way this redbird will fall to the ground in time, a cold stone, and I too will grow cold, and all my line.

Never mind. Mind only this tree in winter and this redbird, this tiny god, all fiery light leading to him and gathered in him, this lord of the sunset, this greeter of the coming dark.

Twilight

I went to a land-grant university, a rural school that students at the rival institution dismissed as a cow college, though I was a junior before I ever saw a single cow there. For someone who had spent her childhood almost entirely outdoors, my college life was unacceptably enclosed. Every day I followed the same brick path from crowded dorm to crowded class to crowded office to crowded cafeteria, and then back to the dorm again. A gentler terrain of fields and ponds and piney woods existed less than a mile from the liberal arts high-rise, but I had no time for idle exploring, for poking about in the scaled-down universe where forestry and agriculture students learned their trade.

One afternoon late in the fall of my junior year, I broke. I had stopped at the cafeteria to grab a sandwich before the dinner crowd hit, hoping for a few minutes of quiet in which to read my literature assignment, the poems of Gerard Manley Hopkins, before my evening shift at the dorm desk. But even with few students present, there was nothing resembling quiet in that cavernous room. The loudspeaker blasted John Cougar's ditty about Jack and Diane, and I pressed my fingers into my ears and hunched low over my book. The sound of my own urgent blood thumping through my veins quarreled with the magnificent sprung rhythm of the poem as thoroughly as Jack and Diane did, and I finally snapped the book closed. My heart was still pounding as I stepped into the dorm lobby, ditched my pack, and started walking. I was headed *out*.

It was a delight to be moving, to feel my body expanding into the larger gestures of the outdoors. What a relief to feel my walk lengthening into a stride and my lungs taking in air by the gulp. I kept walking—past the football stadium, past the sororities—until I came to the red dirt lanes of the agriculture program's experimental fields. Brindled cows turned their unsurprised faces toward me in pastures dotted with hay bales that looked like giant spools of golden thread. The empty bluebird boxes nailed to the fence posts were shining in the slanted light. A red-tailed hawk—the only kind I could name—glided past, calling into the sky.

I caught my breath and walked on, with a rising sense that glory was all around me. Only at twilight can an ordinary mortal walk in light and dark at once—feet plodding through night, eyes turned up toward bright day. It is a glimpse into eternity, that bewildering notion of endless time, where light and dark exist simultaneously.

When the fields gave way to the experimental forest, the wind had picked up, and dogwood leaves were lifting and falling in the light. There are few sights lovelier than leaves being carried on wind. Though that sight was surely common on the campus quad, I had somehow failed to register it. And the swifts wheeling in the sky as evening came on—they would be visible to anyone standing on the sidewalk outside Haley Center, yet I had missed them, too.

There, in that forest, I heard the sound of trees giving themselves over to night. Long after I turned in my paper on Hopkins, long after I was gone myself, this goldengrove unleaving would be releasing its bounty to the wind.

In Which My Grandmother Tells the Story

of the Day She Was Shot

LOWER ALABAMA, 1982

*I*t was the twenty-ninth day of November. I had been sewing and became tired and bored. This was like many days since Mother died in September. She had been such a comfort to me when my husband died in 1977. Now it seemed I had no anchor.

I decided to drive down to our little country store, where I was sure I would find my best friend and her son, who owned it. I had been there about ten minutes when a man came to the door and asked about some oil for his car. Thomas asked him whether he wanted the can with the red label or the can with the green. The man went out to his car and came back with a rifle.

I was sitting in a rocking chair just inside the door to his left. When I looked up, he was pointing the gun at Thomas to his right. I yelled, "Thomas!" The man turned on me and fired into my chest. This gave Thomas time to get his own handgun. He fired twice at the man, killing him instantly.

It seemed ages before anyone could call an ambulance. They also called the sheriff and the coroner. All the way to the hospital I was conscious and in terrific pain. After surgery I had the strangest feeling that there was a ring around me holding me up or protecting me. I'm sure now it was the Lord's presence. I was on all kinds of life supports—breathing machine, heart machine, oxygen, IV, catheter, etc. But I had no thought that I might not live.

I left the hospital on December 23. When the doctors or others *would say, "It's a miracle that you're alive," I always replied, "I know it is a miracle because my God answers prayer."*

All the time during my husband's last illness and then my mother's, I prayed to be strong for them. I wanted to look after them. Then, when they were gone, I thought, Nobody else needs me. *Now I know the Lord wants me for something else, and I'm praying for him to show me what it is.*

Babel

I thought I had escaped the beautiful, benighted South for good when I left Alabama for graduate school in Philadelphia in 1984, though now I can't imagine how this delusion ever took root. At the age of twenty-two, I had never set foot any farther north than Chattanooga, Tennessee. By the time I got to Philadelphia, I was so poorly traveled—and so geographically illiterate—I could not pick out the state of Pennsylvania on an unlabeled weather map on the evening news.

I can't even say why I thought I should get a doctorate in English. The questions that occupy scholars—details of textuality, previously unnoted formative influences, nuances of historical context—held no interest for me. Why hadn't I applied to writing programs instead? Some vague idea about employability, maybe.

When I tell people, if it ever comes up, that I once spent a semester in Philadelphia, a knot instantly forms in the back of my throat, a reminder across thirty years of the panic and despair I felt with every step I took on those grimy sidewalks, with every breath of that heavy, exhaust-burdened air. I had moved into a walkup on a main artery of West Philly, and I lay awake that first sweltering night with the windows open to catch what passed for a breeze, waiting for the sounds of traffic to die down. They never did. All night long, the gears of delivery trucks ground at the traffic light on the corner; four floors down, strangers muttered and swore in the darkness.

Everywhere in the City of Brotherly Love were metaphors

for my own dislocation: a homeless woman squatting in the grocery store parking lot, indifferent to the puddle spreading below her; the sparrows and pigeons, all sepia and brown, that replaced the scolding blue jays and scarlet cardinals I'd left behind; even deep snow, which all my life I had longed to see, was flecked with soot when it finally arrived. I was so homesick for the natural world that I tamed a mouse who lived in my wall, carefully placing stale Cheetos on the floor beyond me, just to feel the creature's delicate feet skittering across my own bare toes.

If I was misplaced in the city, sick with longing for the hidebound landscape I had just stomped away from, shaking its caked red dirt from my sandals, oh, how much more disrupted I felt in my actual classes. The dead languages I was studying—Old English and Latin—were more relevant to my notions of literature than anything I heard in the literary theory course. The aim of the course, at least so far as I could discern it, was to liberate literature from both authorial intent and any claim of independent meaning achieved by close reading. "The text can't mean anything independent of the reader," the professor, a luminary of the field, announced. "Even the word 'mean' doesn't mean anything."

To a person who has wanted since the age of fourteen to be a poet, a classroom in which all the words of the English language have been made bereft of the power to create meaning, or at least a meaning that can be reliably communicated to others, is not a natural home. I was young, both fearful and arrogant, and perhaps I had been praised too often for an inclination to argue on behalf of a cause.

"The word 'mean' doesn't mean anything"—these were fighting words to me. I raised my hand. "Pretend we're in the library, and you're standing on a ladder above me, eye-level with a shelf that holds *King Lear* and *Jane Fonda's Workout*

Book," I said, red-faced and stammering, sounding far less as-sured than I felt. "If I say, 'Hand me down that tragedy,' which book do you reach for?"

The other students in the class, young scholars already versed in the fundamental ideas behind post-structuralist lit-erary theories, must have thought they were listening to Elly May Clampett. They laughed out loud. I never raised my hand again.

Once, not long after I arrived in Philadelphia, a thundering car crash splintered the relative calm of a Sunday afternoon outside my apartment, and the building emptied itself onto the sidewalk as everyone came out to see what happened. I'm not speaking in metaphors when I say that my neighbors were surely as lost as I was: mostly immigrants from somewhere much farther away than Alabama, they couldn't communicate with each other or with me—not because we couldn't agree on the meaning of the words, but because none of the words we knew belonged to the same language.

Bare Ruin'd Choirs

The miserable heat of summer lingered and lingered and lingered, and the drought deepened and deepened and deepened, from moderate to severe to extreme. Most leaves simply curled up from the edges, fading from green to brown before dropping to the ground with hardly a flare of color to remind us that the world is turning, that the world is only a great blue ball rolling down a great glass hill, gaining speed with each rotation.

My favorite season is spring—until fall arrives, and then my favorite season is fall: the seasons of change, the seasons that tell me to wake up, to remember that every passing moment of every careening day is always the last moment, always the very last time, always the only instant I will ever take that precise breath or watch that exact cloud scud across that particular blue of the sky.

How foolish it is for a mortal being to need such reminders, but oh how much easier it is to pay attention when the world beckons, when the world holds out its cupped hands and says, "Lean close. Look at *this*!" This leaf will never again be exactly this shade of crimson. The nestlings in the euonymus just beyond the window will never again be this bald or this blind. Nothing gold can stay.

And yet in winter the bare limbs of the sycamore reveal the mockingbird nest it sheltered all summer, unseen barely a foot above my head, and the night sky spreads out its stars so profusely that the streetlights are only a nuisance, and the

red-tailed hawk fluffs her feathers over her cold yellow feet
and surveys the earth with such stillness I could swear it
wasn't turning at all.

Thanksgiving

Winter break came so early in December that it made no sense to go home for Thanksgiving, no matter how homesick I was. But as the dark nights grew longer and the cold winds blew colder, I wavered. Was it too late? Could I still change my mind?

It was too late. Of course. It was far, far too late. And I had papers to write. I had papers to grade. Also, I had no car, and forget booking a plane ticket so close to the holiday, even if I'd had money to spare for a plane ticket, which on a graduate student's stipend I definitely did not. Amtrak was sold out, and the long, long bus ride seemed too daunting. I would be spending Thanksgiving in Philadelphia, a thousand miles from home.

"I don't think I can stand it here," I said during the weekly call to my parents that Sunday. "I don't know if I can do this."

"Just come home," my father said.

"It's too late." I was crying by then. "It's way too late."

"You can always come home, Sweet," he said. "Even if you marry a bastard, you can always leave him and come on home."

My father intended no irony in making this point. He had never read Thomas Wolfe—might never have heard of Thomas Wolfe. These were words of loving reassurance from a parent to his child, a reminder that as long as he and my mother were alive, there would always be a place in the world for me, a place where I would always belong, even if I didn't always believe I belonged there.

But I wonder now, decades later, if my father's words were

more than a reminder of my everlasting place in the family. I wonder now if they were also an expression of his own longing for the days when all his chicks were still in the nest, when the circle was still closed and the family that he and my mother had made was complete. I was the first child to leave home, but I had given no thought to my parents' own loneliness as they pulled away from the curb in front of my apartment in Philadelphia, an empty U-Haul rattling behind Dad's ancient panel van, for the long drive back to Alabama without me.

I gave no thought to it then, but I think of it all the time now. I think of my father's words across a bad landline connection in 1984 that reached my homesick heart in cold Philadelphia. I think of the twenty-six-hour bus ride into the heart of Greyhound darkness that followed, a desperate journey that got me home in time for the squash casserole and the cranberry relish. I think most of my own happiness, of all the years with a good man and the family we have made together and the absorbing work—everything that followed a single season of loss, and only because I listened to my father. Because I came home.

BLUEBIRD

The Unpeaceable Kingdom

In spring, I used to search for nests. I would part the branches of shrubs and low-limbed trees, peering into their depths for a clump of sticks and string and shredded plastic—the messy structure of a mockingbird's nest. I would squat and look upward for a cardinal's tidy brown bowl. I scanned the ivy climbing the bricks, searching for a hammock tucked into the leaves by house finches. I checked the hanging fern for the vortex tunnel built by a Carolina wren. I watched at my window for blue jays flying into and out of the tree canopy and tried to pinpoint the exact Y-crook in the branches where they'd hidden their young.

For ten years, this was my faithful nesting-season ritual because our little dog, Betty, a feist mix, was hell on fledglings. In her leaping, tree-climbing youth, I took down my feeders and emptied my birdbath, determined not to invite songbirds into the yard. They nested here anyway, perhaps because our lot backs up to a patch of sheltering woods, perhaps because birds will nest more or less anywhere.

I couldn't keep Betty in the house all spring and summer, but I could certainly keep her inside during the few days when new fliers are most vulnerable. But to do that I needed to know when the babies were likely to leave the nest, and to know *that* I needed to find the nests and keep watch over them. If I knew the species of bird on the nest, and I knew the day her eggs hatched, I could make a good guess about when her young would fledge.

The problem with knowing something is that I cannot unknow it. Knowing there are two eggs in the redbird nest means knowing not only an approximate fledge date for the redbird babies but also exactly how many eggs the rat snake ate between yesterday afternoon, when I checked on the mama bird, and this morning, when I found her nest empty. The loss you don't know about is no less a loss, but it costs you nothing and so it causes you no pain.

Human beings are storytelling creatures, craning to see the crumpled metal in the closed-off highway lane, working from the moment the traffic slows to construct a narrative from what's left behind. But our tales, even the most tragic ones, hinge on specificity. The story of one drowned Syrian boy washed up in the surf keeps us awake at night with grief. The story of four million refugees streaming out of Syria seems more like a math problem.

The grief of the failed nest echoes in an entirely different register, but it is still a grief. In Tennessee it's common for cardinals to nest twice in a season, hatching between two and five eggs each time, but few of their young will survive. The world is not large enough to contain so many cardinals, and predators must eat, too, and feed their own young. It should not trouble me to know the sharp-eyed crow will feed its babies with any hatchlings it steals from the cardinals, but I have watched day after day as the careful redbird constructed a sturdy nest in the laurel, and I have calculated how many days and nights she has sat upon those eggs, how many trips she has made to the nest to feed the babies, how many times she has sheltered them through a downpour. Day after day after day.

After Betty died, I stopped checking my yard for nests in springtime, but my eyes are tuned now to the signs of nesting—to the male blue jay feeding the female on the limb just past my deck, to the tufted titmouse plucking loose fur from my surviving dog's haunches as he sleeps in the sun, to the chickadee gathering moss from the deepest shade at the back of the yard. And I can't unsee the nests they build.

It's wrongheaded to interfere in nature when something is neither unnatural nor likely to upset the natural order. I can't help myself. A crow lands too close to the redbird nest, and I rush outside with my broom. A red wasp chases a brooding bluebird from the nest box, and I rub soap into the wood of the birdhouse roof. It's humiliating, all the ways I've interfered.

In recent weeks I've watched a pair of Carolina chickadees building a nest in the bluebird box outside my office window. When a bluebird arrived and tried to evict them, I stood outside in the pouring rain and put up another nest box a few yards away. The bluebird gave it no notice, but he stopped pestering the chickadees, and all seemed well. Then a house wren showed up.

One year a wren killed a chickadee nestling on my watch, so when I heard the unmistakable trilling of a house wren calling for a mate, I looked reflexively toward the bluebird box where the chickadee was sitting on five speckled eggs. There was the brown wren, a feathered fusion of music and violence, perched right on the roof of the birdhouse and singing a song that could only be a territorial claim. The new nest box, empty and pristine, was ten paces away, but that one didn't interest him. I got up from my desk, went outside, and walked straight toward him until he flew away.

Two days later the chickadee was gone, her nest empty, and I watched from the window as two male bluebirds fought over the box, leaping into the air and knocking each other to the ground. In the underbrush at the edge of the yard, the wren was still singing.

March

I lived less than a hundred miles from Selma, Alabama, but I was three years old on the day in 1965 that came to be known as Bloody Sunday. Twenty years later I knew next to nothing still. I knew state troopers had clubbed six hundred peaceful African Americans as they knelt to pray for courage on the Edmund Pettus Bridge, but I had never heard of Jimmie Lee Jackson, murdered for believing in the right to vote. I didn't know that the idea for the march first took hold when someone said they should carry the body of Jimmie Lee Jackson to Montgomery and lay it on the capitol steps so George Wallace could see what preserving white supremacy actually looked like.

In 1985, knowing so very little, I walked in the commemorative march from Selma to Montgomery on the twentieth anniversary of Bloody Sunday. I wish I could claim it as a long-held plan, but I hadn't meant to march. I had driven south with two friends to join in the rally, to hear the speeches after the march was all over. But far outside town, just past Prattville and the sign warning travelers to GO TO CHURCH OR THE DEVIL WILL GET YOU, the northbound lanes of I-65 had been closed to automobiles and our side turned into a two-lane thruway. Drivers in both directions were confused, or just curious, and traffic was hood-to-trunk, hardly moving. Clearly we were never going to make it into Montgomery for the rally, so we pulled over and parked. Just then the first group of marchers arrived on the other side of the road, heading into the city.

They were exuberant, singing and laughing, walking hand in hand or with their arms around each other's necks. Some of them looked across the median blooming with crimson clover and saw us leaning against our car. We waved. They waved back.

Then a handful of them were beckoning, and without even pausing to look at one another, my friends and I were dodging between the slow-moving cars and heading across the median. Seeing us coming, the entire group sent up a cheer; several of them—those closest to the spot where we joined the line—hugged us, draping their arms across our shoulders and singing at the top of their lungs the words to a song I'd never heard before.

More than three decades later, I can still exactly recall the smile on one older woman's face as she reached out to grab my sleeve and pull me into the throng of marchers. I can still smell the damp clover in the median. I can still feel my burning cheeks and my thumping heart. But no matter how joyful, how hopeful, I suddenly felt—no matter how desperately I wanted to—they were singing a song I didn't recognize, and I couldn't add my voice to theirs. I could not sing along.

Still

I pause to check the milkweed, and a caterpillar halts mid-bite, its face still lowered to the leaf.

I walk down my driveway at dusk, and the cottontail under the pine tree freezes, not a single twitch of ear or nose.

On the roadside, the doe stands immobile, as still as the trees that rise above her. My car passes; her soft nose doesn't quiver. Her soft flanks don't rise or fall. A current of air stirs only the hairs at the very tip of her tail.

I peek between the branches of the holly bush, and the redbird nestling looks straight at me, motionless, unblinking.

—

Every day the world is teaching me what I need to know to be in the world.

—

In the stir of too much motion:
>   Hold still.
>   Be quiet.
>   Listen.

Homesick

I left Philadelphia, but in between the determination and the act were many humiliations: endless weeping, an illness I couldn't seem to shake, incompletes in all my courses. I actually went back to Philadelphia in January, determined to start all over again, but forty-eight hours later I bought a ticket on a train heading south. When I lurched into the club car near midnight, I was not surprised to find a guy in back playing hobo songs on a harmonica. I had become the tragic heroine in a Willie Nelson movie.

I could have looked for more congenial courses, shifted the focus of my study. Instead I spent the semester as a typist for Kelly Girl, as a substitute teacher at my old high school, as the lone night clerk at a Catholic bookstore. On the way home from work, whatever "work" happened to be that day, I would stop at the video store and rent *Harold and Maude*. I always checked the new-release shelf just in case anything more appealing had come in, but nothing ever did. Night after night it was *Harold and Maude*.

I pretended to everyone, including myself, that I would be going back to school; as soon as I felt better, I would complete the final papers I owed my first-semester professors and be ready to start again in the fall. My parents held their tongues. On the way to the kitchen late at night, my father would walk through the dark living room, pause a moment, and ask, "Whatcha watching, Sweet?"

"*Harold and Maude*."

"Ah."

Clearly I was going nowhere, least of all to Philadelphia.

In June, back at my old college for my brother's graduation, I hid from the professors who had written my graduate school recommendations, the ones who had been so pleased to aid my escape. But walking through the experimental fields I'd stalked in despair only two years earlier, I ran into my former Latin teacher, the kind of old-school professor who teaches an overload unpaid—convening class at seven in the morning, before any other classes began, five mornings a week, for more than two years—because the university wouldn't schedule a Latin literature course for only four students. I ended up sitting on his porch for an hour, lamenting the failure of self-knowledge that had led to my miserable fate.

"Don't go back," he said. "Go with Billy to South Carolina instead. Get your master's in writing while he gets his in art. Write poems instead of papers."

Sitting on that front porch in the heat of an Alabama summer, with grasshoppers buzzing in the ag fields just across the road and bluebirds swooping off the fence posts to snatch them up, I considered the alternate future he was laying before me: a life of poems. It was a lifeline to a life.

Revelation

The fog comes on little cat feet, as everyone knows, but the fog does not sit on silent haunches except in poems. In the world, the fog is busy. It hides stalking cat and scratching sparrow alike. It blunts sharp branches, unbends crooked twigs, makes of every tree a gentler shape in a felted shade of green. Deep in the forest, it wakes the hidden webs into a landscape of dreams, laying jewels, one by one, along every tress and filament. The morning sun burns in the sky as it must, but the world belongs to the fog for now, and the fog is busy masking and unmasking, shrouding what we know and offering to our eyes what we have failed to see.

FIG

Nature Abhors a Vacuum

In South Carolina I found my way back to myself. All it took was an ant swarm on a glittering chain-link fence, thousands of new wings glinting like silver in the sun. An escaped hawk trailing its zoo leash, joyfully killing pigeons on the state capitol steps. The heart-tripping sight of a brown water snake coiled in a tree in the Congaree swamp. The sulfurous scent of a dogwood tree outside my window split in half by a lightning bolt. The whinny of a screech owl in the dark. The taste of fresh figs.

Two by Two

In springtime the chickadees bring bits of moss to the nest box; and the redbird feeds his mate, seed by seed; and the bluebird carefully inspects every nest site her suitor escorts her to, hoping one will meet her standards; and the red-tailed hawks circle the sky on opposite sides of the same arc; and the bachelor mockingbird sings all night long. He will keep on singing until someone accepts his song.

The Kiss

The bench was hard, curved and flat in all the wrong places. The grass was too damp to lie in, and the night swarmed with mosquitoes the likes of which can be found only in a river basin in South Carolina—large and insistent and more numerous even than the roaches. The slippery Skin So Soft I'd applied hours earlier in lieu of DEET was sticky by then and doing nothing to repel mosquitoes, despite my own best organic intentions. My favorite teaching skirt was getting ruined—hopelessly wrinkled, flecked with flaking green paint, and smeared with bird droppings. None of these things registered with me.

But they must have registered somehow, at some point, because decades later I recall them all perfectly—the feel of the bunched fabric of that long cotton skirt, the salty-sweet smell of Skin So Soft mingled with human blood from slapped mosquitoes, the wet grass licking at our ankles and pooling at our feet, the way the seat of the bench was too deep and cut off circulation to my knees. I was Edith Ann in the old *Laugh-In* skit, my legs sticking out, too short to touch the ground. I was also nothing like a child.

We were alone in the back of an unlighted pocket park, hardly more than a vacant lot with a rusty swing set in the middle, located somewhere between the attic apartment where I lived with my brother and the classroom where I was teaching undergraduates to write. It was already getting dark when a man in my graduate program—a friend who might be on the verge of becoming something more than a friend, although who can ever say for sure about a thing like that so early on, when the question first forms itself into a question?—had offered to walk me home.

We hadn't walked far before suddenly neither of us was in any hurry to get me there. I don't remember how we drifted from the sidewalk to the bench, or how we even knew the bench was there in the dark, or whether we wandered over to it while there was still light in the lengthening April day and simply stayed till the light ran out. I don't remember where I set the tapestry bag my mother had made to carry all those ungraded papers back and forth on my long walk to class. I don't remember taking off my shoes, or hitching up my skirt, or whether I was hungry, or how we started kissing. All I remember is the kiss that lasted for hours in the dark, a kiss that ended only when the darkness had gone from black to almost gray and was moving on toward dawn.

I Didn't Choose

The night after my husband and I brought our first child home from the hospital, my mother and father cooked a celebratory meal. I looked around the festive table, happy to be home. I was grateful for the loving man I had married, for the loving parents who had raised me, for the new little person who had come into the world in the midst of all that love.

Hot tears welled up so suddenly my eyes blurred. One drop fell onto my plate and quivered in the candlelight: a miniature dome of inexplicable sadness.

My husband noticed first. "Honey!" he said. "What is it?"

"I don't know." The tears poured down.

Maybe it was hormones at first, but weeks passed and still I cried. I cried because it hurt to nurse. I cried because I had no instinct for baby talk and felt foolish trying. I cried because I missed myself. I would look at my puffy face in the mirror. *What has happened to me?*

What happened to me: depression, mastitis—raging infections over and over again—loneliness, a baby who needed to be held all the time, and it never crossed my mind that he was simply cold. It was January, and the world was full of microbes. The pediatrician told me not to take him out until his immune system was stronger, so I fed him, and I held him, and everything else fell away. We moved from bed to sofa and back again, day after day after day. I smelled of sour milk and vomit. My hair hung limp in my eyes because I was too tired to lift a hand and push it behind my ears.

At the baby's eight-week checkup, the pediatrician looked at her clipboard. "Are you still nursing?"

My throat closed up. By the time she looked at me an instant later, tears were falling onto the baby's head, one fat drop after another. She put the clipboard down. "Tell me about it," she said.

I told her about the midnight trips to the emergency room, my breasts on fire, my teeth chattering from fever. I told her my baby was always, always hungry. I told her I did nothing all day but feed him. I had to bite a dry washrag to keep from crying out.

The doctor leaned forward and put her hand on my arm. "The best mother is a happy mother," she said. "Give that baby a bottle."

Overnight my baby stopped crying, surfeited for the first time in his hungry life. He would drop off to sleep, his whole body at ease, arms and legs as limp as a rag doll's. He slept and slept. The days grew warmer and longer. I pushed his stroller to the park, and we watched the older children play. All day long he smiled at me with a look of love so rapturous I felt unworthy. No one had ever loved me that purely. As a girl, I was as wholly loved as any child on earth, and I was sure this baby loved me even more than that. And the love he felt for me was nothing at all to my love for him.

But I missed my teaching job. I missed having people to talk to. I missed spending my days considering the greatest literature produced in my language. My baby slept and slept, and I was restless. Finally I buckled his tiny self into the car with an absurd amount of gear and drove home to Birmingham.

"You loved your job, too," I said to my mother, who had once been a home-demonstration agent with the county extension service. Before I was born, she had traveled the back roads of Lower Alabama carrying pattern books in her trunk, stopping at community houses and church fellowship halls to show the rural women gathered there what the latest fashions looked like, to teach them the latest sewing techniques. Later, she had chafed so much at the monotony of life with young children that her frustration was clear to me even as a child. "You talk about that job all the time. Why did you decide to stay home?"

"I didn't *decide*," she said instantly, with a bitterness I had never heard in her voice before. "I didn't *choose*." She had been forced to resign as soon as she was visibly pregnant with me. By law the mothers of children too young for school could not work for the state of Alabama.

I remembered, then, a time when my mother went to work in my father's office, though she could neither type nor take dictation—and suddenly it made sense to me. My mother had chosen work, even work she was not qualified to do, over staying home with her children. I thought of how desperate I felt during my seemingly endless maternity leave. If staying home was this hard for me, with an end point in sight, supported by my very culture, how much harder must it have been for her in 1961?

In another age, or in another place, my wildly creative mother might have been very different. She was a woman who designed and made her own clothes, who loved to jitterbug, whose laugh was so infectious even strangers turned, searching for the source of her joy. Perhaps she would have gone to art school, thrown ecstatic parties. Perhaps she would have been happier in even a small-town life, instead of retreating every afternoon into a darkened room, curtains closed against the heat. Perhaps she wouldn't have needed her little girl to tiptoe in with a blue pill and a glass of water in the gloom.

In Bruegel's *Icarus*, for Instance

GULF SHORES, 1993

It was our son's first trip to the beach, and I had dressed him in a swimsuit for children who cannot swim: it reached from his throat to his knees, blocks of buoyant foam sewn into pockets circling his chest and belly—the soft toddler belly that swelled with each breath. "He looks like a suicide bomber," my husband said. In those days we still joked about suicide bombers here, where such creatures seemed almost imaginary, dwelling on the other side of the world.

"I don't want him to be afraid of the ocean," I said.

"He's not afraid," my husband said. "You're afraid."

So I settled our boy on my hip and carried him straight into the water—ankle-deep, knee-deep, hip-deep, waist-deep. He kicked his fat feet and his squat toes. I turned to look at my husband, triumphant. He was already striding toward us from shore, his long legs pushing through the waves.

I never saw the one that rose up behind me, the one that crashed over my head, knocked me over, and snatched our baby from my arms. I remember clearly the sudden silence beneath the brown water, though surely a churning ocean could not have been silent. I remember my own hair dragging the sand through that murk—however improbably, decades later, I still see my hair swaying against the floor of the sea.

When I finally found my feet, when I finally pushed my streaming hair away from my face and wiped the stinging water from my eyes, the absurd swimsuit had done its job, if poorly: our boy had risen, too, but yards away, bobbing upside down on the surface of the spent wave as it pulled back from shore, his white legs scissoring the air.

My husband reached him first, swim-team strokes of decades past closing the gap in a moment, and scooped our baby up and carried him to shore, those small lungs coughing out all the water in the world.

By the time I reached them on the sand, they were smiling. No tragedy had touched us, no catastrophe but the near loss I still carry—the shadow that, even now, I cannot set down.

All Birds?

Except for the splayed wing feathers, the robin in the street was unrecognizable. "What dis?" my three-year-old asked, squatting to peer at it.

"That's a bird," I said.

Toddlers are severe enforcers of norms, and my middle child was not having this explanation. "Dat not a bird," he said. "It not flying."

"It's a dead bird," I said. "It can't fly anymore because a car ran over it."

"Dat bird dead," he repeated. "Have a little trouble flying."

Every day, for nearly a week, we had to walk down the street to look at the tatters of this unlucky robin. My boy was clearly trying to work something out, but he didn't ask any more questions. He just looked at the bird for a bit and then walked on. "You dead," he whispered once, squatting in front of the bird. "You dead. You not a bird."

Then one day he looked at me. A new thought had come to him: "All birds die?" he asked.

I tried to put the best possible face on a hard truth about this lovely world. "All birds die, but first they build a nest and lay eggs and feed their babies worms and fly and fly and fly."

"All birds die," he repeated. His eyes filled up with tears.

A few days later he was lying on the floor beside our dog. "Scout will die?" he asked, almost absently. I told him Scout would die one day, too. The next question came immediately:

"All dogs die?" And then he was off. Every day became a crash course in the reach of mortality:

"All fish die?"

"All squirrels die?"

"All teachers die?"

"All dese people in the grocery store die?"

"All mommies die?"

I answered his questions without hedging. I didn't want my three-year-old staring into the abyss, but I wouldn't lie to him either. But then he asked the question that made me want to lie and lie again and keep lying forever: "I will die?" he said, his voice quavering. "I will be dead?"

HONEYSUCKLE

Metastatic

A starling lifts itself from the wire, and a thousand starlings follow, spiraling into the sky. They are pouring in from the treetops, from the roofline—the sky is roiling with wheeling birds, each one an animate cell.

In spring the bush honeysuckle shelters the bluebird fledglings and the brown wrens. In summer the honeysuckle flowers open to the eager bees. In fall the honeysuckle feeds the cedar waxwings, who cling to the bending stems and pass the berries to flock mates who cannot reach. In winter the honeysuckle waits, gathering itself to spring forth, to wrap its roots around what rightly belongs. To choke it out.

Behold the fearsome lionfish, its spines fanning out like a mane, its stripes an underwater circus act, its translucent fins an exotic veil. Behold the gorgeous lionfish floating unmolested in foreign waters, passing near the small creatures at home here and gulping them down, whole.

The lymph nodes are clusters of grapes, ripe, though there will be no wine. They swell and swell with cancer, malignant cells spilling over and spreading, clinging and growing, spilling and spreading and clinging and growing and spilling and spreading and spreading and spreading.

Death-Defying Acts

Terminal illness was perched on the house like a vulture. We walked beneath its hunched presence as though it weren't there, the way you try not to make eye contact with a stranger who's openly staring.

Need governed our days. My father needed help, and my mother needed help with the helping, and I needed to help in a way that allowed me to do my work and also take care of my family. Dad had chemotherapy every other Wednesday. On Thursday, Mom would pack the car and drive them to my house, 182 miles away. My oldest son would sleep on the futon in my office, my husband and I would sleep in our son's double bed, and my parents would sleep in our room, the only room in the house with its own bathroom. Twelve days later, Mom would drive them home. They would sleep in their own bed and wake up in time to head to the clinic for another round of chemo. The next day it was back to my house again.

During one of those visits, Dad suddenly remembered that the circus was coming to town. Not to Nashville, the town where I live, but to Birmingham, the town where he lived.

"You know, I've always wanted to go to the circus," he said one day, out of nowhere.

"You should go, Dad," I said. "Of course."

"The boys would love the circus," Dad said. "You know how much they would love the circus."

Oh.

This wasn't part of the last-chance bucket list at all. This was another trope, one that involved indelible images of grandfatherly largesse. It was a hedge against oblivion, a way to be remembered.

I spent much of my father's final illness in a state of exhausted resignation, but the flip side of resignation is fury, and fury sometimes found its way through the cracks in my splintered life. My husband, my children, my parents, my siblings—they were the entire bounded universe to me, and one of them was being pulled away forever. But lying under the covers in my own bed, the bed I almost never slept in, I knew my beloved father was asking me to give up two of the only four days every month when I had my own little family to myself. He was asking me to give up my only near respite from cancer.

"No." I said it flatly, a belligerent word left over from toddlerhood or the year I was thirteen. "I'm sorry, Dad. We can't go to Birmingham to see the circus two days from now. We have stuff to do here. We have plans."

"Oh," he said, sounding slightly surprised. "Oh." Then, recovering, not quite pleading but trying one more time: "You know the kids would love the circus." .

"I know they would, Dad, but I wouldn't," I said.

I was forty years old—a writer, a wife, a parent—but I still thought of my father's love, of his unshakable belief in me, as the surest protection against my own inconsequence. "You can always come home," he had said. "Even if you marry a bastard, you can always leave him and come on home." But that home had long since ceased to exist, reduced to a sour-smelling shell holding whole shelves of medication and a trash can for my father to cough into as phlegm built in his throat. Becoming responsible for his care and my mother's equilibrium probably meant I had been hauled into a new kind of adulthood unaware, even if I wasn't behaving like an adult. "No," I said. "I don't want to go to the circus."

At the time, I still thought I could find a way to bear the idea of a world without my father in it. What I couldn't bear was any more suffering. I wanted my father to act like my father, damn it, even to the end. Was that my reason for refusing to let him take my children to the circus? By acting like a child myself, was I trying to force him to become my vibrant father again and not a frightened old man who wanted only to be remembered as a hero by his grandsons?

"Well, put it on the calendar for next time then," he said, backing down. "The circus comes back in two years, and I want to take the boys next time."

Next time.

For my terminally ill father, there would be no next time, and I knew it. And he knew I knew it. We were going to the circus.

In Praise of the Unlovely World

Teetering between despair and terror, alarmed by the perils that threaten the planet, defeated in imagining any real way to help, I'm tempted to turn away, to focus on what is lovely in a broken world: moonlight on still water, the full-body embrace of bumblebees in the milkweed flowers, the first dance of the newlyweds, whose eyes never leave each other in all their turnings on the gleaming floor.

But even destruction can remind us of all the ways the world has found of working itself out. Someone steps on a cockroach on the dark sidewalk, and by morning the ants have arrived to carry it off, infinitesimal bit by bit. A car hits a doe on a country road, and the flies share it with the glossy vultures. A beer can tossed carelessly from the car window glints like treasure in the sunlight. Even in its shining, it is already in the long grip of corrosion—eighty years, a hundred—that will take it down to fertile soil.

Chokecherry

When I think of the first time my heart broke, the summer I was fourteen, I don't think at all of the boy who broke it. I think of walking around and around our block, desolate among the ubiquitous dogwoods, weeping as though I had invented heartbreak all by myself. I think of my father, standing at the end of the driveway, cracked where a chokecherry root had pushed up the concrete so it buckled like a fault line, waiting for me to come home. Each time I passed, still crying, he would kick his toe against the break and try to look as though he were considering the maintenance problem at hand. He'd smile at me, and though I couldn't have known it then, it was the smile of someone whose own heart was breaking too.

On the night my father died, he was lying in the big bed in the corner room where he had slept for thirty years. Listing beside him was a slanting bookcase he had built himself, and on one of its shelves—right at eye level—was a picture of my mother on their wedding day, and one of me in my First Communion gown, and pictures of my brother and sister, of the commonplace life of our family. All through the long night it took my dying father to die, I lay beside him, holding his hand and looking at those pictures.

He was long past seeing by then, and each breath was a gasp that shook his whole body, but still the breaths kept coming. *Please die,* I thought, every time there was a pause between the shuddering exhale and the next desperate, grasping breath. *Please die. Please let this be the last one. Please die.*

I didn't see it when the last breath finally came, when my strong, sheltering father ceased for the first time in my lucky life to be my father. I didn't see it because I had lifted my eyes from his face just once, turned for only a moment to the window on the other side of the room, wondering when the light would come.

RABBIT

He Is Not Here

One year, helping me in the garden in early spring, my middle son inadvertently uncovered a cottontail nest tucked beneath the rosemary. The baby rabbits seemed hopelessly vulnerable: thumb-sized creatures, eyes still closed, without any shelter from the cold March rains.

And yet their nest under the rosemary plant was a snug nursery. Their mother had scooped out a shallow hollow in the soil and lined it thickly with her own fur; more fur lay on top of the babies; and on top of that was a final layer of leaves and pine straw and dried rosemary needles. It was impossible to distinguish the nest from the jumble of dead vegetation that had piled up during fall and winter. And as my son pointed out, the location of the nest was ideal: to predators it would smell exactly like rosemary and not at all like rabbit. We tucked the babies in again and left the bed unweeded till they were safely out of the nest and on their own.

I've been desultory about weeding in springtime ever since. Spring is the time, Gerard Manley Hopkins noted, "when weeds, in wheels, shoot long and lovely and lush," and there's another reason for waiting to clear out my flower beds: the neighborhood bees are busy among the flowering weeds long before the perennials bloom. Who can resist the names of wildflowers—fleabane and henbit and purple deadnettle and creeping Charlie?

Finally, though, the day comes when there can be no more waiting or the weeds will choke out all the flowers I planted on purpose. That day came one long Easter weekend. My reliable garden helper was away in college, and

I worked alone, gingerly, careful to watch for signs of a nest. There was nothing beneath the rosemary but mock strawberry vines. Moving from bed to bed, I hauled away weeds by the wheelbarrow-load.

Then, in the next-to-last bed, I tugged up some purple deadnettle growing around the fragrant skeleton of last year's oregano, and what came away in my hand was a tuft of rabbit fur. The nest was empty but so newly vacated as to be entirely intact, an absence exactly shaped to denote an ineffable presence.

Hypochondria

On another day I wouldn't have noticed the lump. My breasts have always been bumpy, and my doctor has never seemed concerned—"busy breasts," she calls them. I didn't even bother checking them in the shower: If everything's a lump, then what's the point?

That day I was anxious but also bored. We were waiting for the test results that would tell us whether a hellish bout of radiation and chemo had killed the cancer growing in my father's esophagus. Pacing the oncology hallway, I picked up a plastic card that explained how to do a breast self-exam, and I was still holding that card when the doctor came into the examining room and clipped some scans onto a light board. He pointed to a cluster of ghostly white orbs that were swollen lymph nodes. He pointed to a dark spot on my father's liver. The cancer wasn't gone. The cancer was spreading.

Being in the presence of death can transform otherwise reasonable people into augurs, bargaining with the cosmos: "If I stop being blasé about my health, will you promise not to kill me?" Holding that card, I vowed to call for an appointment the moment I got home. If I didn't want my own children to face the agony of losing a parent too soon, it was time to let a medical professional decide which of the myriad lumps in my breasts were normal and which were not.

The nurse practitioner was kind. As she gently rubbed and prodded and kneaded, I told her about my father's illness. Dad had always been the one person who could make me feel both completely protected and certain of my own strength. It was hard to separate what was happening to him from what was happening to me. I was surely wasting her time, I said, but I wanted to be safe.

She nodded. Then she said, "Oops, there's a mass."

A word like "mass"—just by itself, not even to mention the dying father taking up the dread chambers of the mind—has a way of stripping all logic from a conversation. The nurse told me, repeatedly, that this mass did not feel to her like cancer, that 80 percent of breast lumps, even suspicious ones, turn out to be nothing, that it was not time to start planning my funeral.

To a person with a mass in her breast, a word like "funeral" is a dirty bomb, exploding into cutting fragments that lodge deep in the reptilian brain. By the time I'd had a mammogram and an ultrasound and a biopsy, by the time I'd met with the cheerful surgeon who said he wasn't worried but still wanted to see me again in three months, I knew I was dying.

Over and over again during my father's illness and for more than a year after his death, the pattern was both primitive and modern: a lump, an inconclusive test, more doctors, more tests. Each time the mammogram was stable, the ultrasound fine, the biopsy normal. I was not relieved. I would brood about the cancer they didn't catch. My father was dying, and I was surely dying too.

When decorations went on sale after the holidays, I would think, *I might not live to see next Christmas*, and buy nothing. Every headache was a tumor, every bout of indigestion stomach cancer. Stress and grief colluded to produce ever more symptoms, and each new symptom required a test: ultrasound, colonoscopy, endoscopy, colposcopy, EKG, blood test after blood test after blood test. They all turned out fine, but I knew I wasn't fine. I was dying.

When I didn't die, however, and then didn't die some more, I came one day to understand: I wasn't dying; I was grieving. I wasn't dying. Not yet.

The Shape the Wreckage Takes

Barefoot and still in her nightgown, my mother comes into my kitchen at lunchtime and looks down the steps to the family room. Her eyes are swollen and red, as they have been for all the weeks since my father's death. My four-year-old, the youngest, is playing on the wooden floor alone. He is pushing small metal cars off the bottom step and watching them crash into each other. This game requires all his concentration. He seems to have some plan for the shape the wreckage must take. He does not hear, or at least does not acknowledge, his grandmother. "Hi, honey," she says.

"Hi, Wibby," he says, not looking up. Then, "Granddaddy played cars with me."

Whenever my mother told this story in the years to come, it was meant to be an example of how God had made a terrible mistake. It was another reason in the long list of reasons she always marshaled for why, if she and my father could not have gone into the next world together, then at least she should have been the one to go first. Confirmation that a bad bargain had somehow been struck.

But my four-year-old's remark was not a rebuke. It had nothing to do with her. He was a little boy, and he was still finding out all the places where his grandfather had been but would be no longer. This new absence was a missing tooth, the hole he couldn't help probing with his tongue. His grandfather had played cars with him. His grandfather had read books to him. His grandfather had walked around the block with him, holding his hand.

Witches' Broom

My great-grandfather ordered a sprig of the Dr. Van Fleet rambling rose shortly after it was introduced in 1910. When my grandparents married in 1930, my grandmother brought a rooted cutting to her new home a few miles down the road. Years later, when we moved to Birmingham, my mother brought a cutting with us, and later still, I brought one to Nashville.

I don't grow roses because of all the spraying invariably involved, but the Dr. Van Fleet is an absurdly hardy exception. For almost two decades, ours withstood countless droughts and Nashville cold snaps, needed no chemicals at all, and seemed impervious to insects. Every year it sheltered at least one cardinal's nest, and those baby birds always made it safely into the world. (A bird's nest built among the thorny canes of an antique rambling rose is about as predator-proof as a nest can be.)

Then my Dr. Van Fleet contracted rose rosette virus, a fatal and incurable disease. First discovered among wild roses in 1941, it is now widespread in the United States. The virus is carried on the wind by mites, and the popularity of Knock Out roses, which are particularly vulnerable to RRV, seems to have hastened its spread.

The telltale sign of this disease is the witches' broom—stems of disfigured new growth clustered at the end of a rose cane. With a rambling rose, if you know what you're looking for, you can sometimes see the beginnings of a classic witches'-broom formation in time to dig the diseased canes out, but I didn't know what I was looking for the year my rose first got sick. By the next spring, when only a few canes leafed out, there was almost nothing left of the Dr. Van Fleet but thorns.

Having no choice, we cut it down and dug up as many of the roots as possible, heartsick. All my beloved elders were gone, and the rose I had hoped to pass along to my children was gone now too.

Rambling roses are easy to propagate in springtime: to create a new rosebush, you place a pot of dirt beneath a cane and set a brick on top of the cane to hold it against the soil in the pot. Beneath the brick, the rose will put down roots. After a few weeks, you can remove the brick, cut the pot free from the main cane, and carry it to a new place in the yard. A rose propagated in this way is genetically identical to the original rose. In essence, you have only one rose, though it is growing in two different places. My own Dr. Van Fleet was the very same rose my great-grandfather first planted in 1910.

The year before I lost the Dr. Van Fleet, I had started a potted rose and forgotten about it beneath the tangle of canes. When I discovered it again in cutting down the rose, I assumed it too would be afflicted with the witches' broom. I kept it just in case I was wrong, but I set it far from any other flowers in my yard and never planted it. Still in its pot three years later, at age 107, it bloomed.

You Can't Go Home Again

My grandfather was tired of being hot in the summertime and cold in the winter. Perhaps he was getting a bit muddled, too, but in 1970 my grandmother didn't try to stop him when he decided to sell the big house, the homeplace, where he had lived almost every year of his life. It was his house to sell if he wanted to, according to my grandmother, and he wanted to: "I have carried in wood and carried out ashes all my life, and I'm tired of it," he said. "I'd like to get a place we can heat and cool."

The man who bought the big house promptly sold the timber off the back acreage for more than he'd paid my grandfather for the whole place, and then he sold the house for yet again more money than he'd paid. My heartbroken mother could hardly bring herself to forgive her father, old though he was and so feeble. He had given away her family home, a safe place for the generations, and all for a cinder-block double-wide with a concrete driveway and central air.

By the time my grandmother died in 2006, she had been with my mother in Birmingham for more than ten years and blind for longer than that, and I hope she never saw the changes in the big house, though they unfolded barely half a mile down the road from the tiny house my grandfather had built for their old age. Her rose border: gone, including the Dr. Van Fleet she'd brought from her childhood home. The floorboards of the front porch: gone, replaced with a concrete slab. The gnarled old tree that grew plums swollen and almost black with juice: gone. And gone, too: all the red wasps drunk on plum juice fermenting in the Alabama sun.

We brought our grandmother back home to Lower Alabama in a box. After the church funeral, my brother and sister and I left our mother at the potluck in the old school-house where our grandmother had once taught and walked over to look at the big house. The first thing we noticed was how small it was.

Ashes, Part One

For a long time, Mom wouldn't tell us where she kept Dad's ashes. "That's between your father and me," she would say. Given her unconventional taxonomies, we knew she might have stashed them anywhere. And given her tendency toward hoarding, we also knew they would be hard to tell from detritus. Once, trying to restore order on a trip home, I found the urn in a box under the old claw-foot table. It was surrounded by mouse droppings, junk mail, outdated newspapers, and garage-sale rolls of fabric that my mother had left on the dining room floor. The next time I went home, the urn was gone.

Years later, after Mom had moved to Nashville and we finally talked her into putting the Birmingham house on the market, it dawned on my sister that she might have accidentally sold the urn at our own garage sale, the one designed to unload all of Mom's geegaws. I didn't think it was possible, but how could we be sure? It wasn't like we could say, "Hey, Mom, we can't find Dad, and there's a chance Lori just sold him to a stranger. Thoughts?"

On a road trip to Lower Alabama to bury our aunt, my sister tried again: "Don't you think it's time to do something about Dad's ashes?"

"That's none of your business," Mom said. "I have a plan for us both, but it's just between Daddy and me."

My sister saw an opening: "But after you die, won't we need to know where Dad is to make this plan work?"

Mom gave in: "OK, he's on the bottom shelf of the guest room closet."

"Great. Now, what's the plan?"

"The family plot is full, but y'all can take a posthole digger down there in the middle of the night and stick me and Daddy in the ground near Mimi and Granddaddy," she said. "I want to go home."

Be Not Afraid

Early in their courtship, my parents knew a little girl who could not pronounce my mother's given name, Olivia, and called her Wibby instead. Wibby became my father's pet name for her, the shorthand he used to summon their days of flirtation. Even during hardships, times of deep worry or sorrow, there was always that echo of their early romance passing back and forth between them. Whenever he heard her laughing—even from another room, having no idea of what had amused her—he couldn't help laughing too. After she started a floral business, he would help with the big orders by copying every move she made: if she added a daisy to the center right of her arrangement, he would add a daisy to the center right of his. When Dad brought home a midlife motorcycle, Mom bought a leather jacket and climbed on back.

During the two and a half years Dad was sick with cancer, Mom left his side only long enough to walk from their room to the kitchen for anything he thought, however fretfully, might settle his churning stomach, and when he died she was lost. Her children, her friends, her church, her flower beds, her sewing projects—none of them offered comfort in the face of cavernous grief.

She had grown up during the Depression on a peanut farm in Lower Alabama, miles from the nearest library. For the first seventy-one years of her life, she had no feeling at all for stories as a source of pleasure or solace, and I never saw her read a book. Then, months after my father died, she went to the library to check out Jane Austen's *Pride and Prejudice* because she'd seen the BBC miniseries a dozen times already and had fallen in love with Mr. Darcy. And that's how, overnight it seemed, she also fell in love with reading. In Regency England she found an entire absorbing world, a grand love story she recognized, though she had never been to Great Britain—had, in fact, rarely left Alabama.

After that it was *Emma*, and *Sense and Sensibility*, and the rest of Austen. Then came other books from the same period and love stories from any era, until finally it was almost anything. During the nine years she lived beyond my father, Mom read comic novels and mysteries, romances and tragedies, and every knockoff Jane Austen novel she could find, no matter how scandalous with twenty-first-century details. ("I couldn't believe it when Mr. Darcy took Elizabeth on the *dining room table!*" she once said.) For Mom, alone in a silent house, these characters must at times have seemed more real to her than even family. In her last years, she lived across the street from my family, and I often checked in midmorning to find her still asleep. "My book was getting so good I had to stay up all night to finish," she would say.

Just before she died, I took her to the emergency room for what was clearly a kidney stone. She had suffered kidney stones before, and the symptoms this time were obvious, but the nurse could give her nothing for the pain until a doctor saw her, and the only doctor there that day was busy with other patients. For more than two hours, the nurse would check in, Mom would ask for pain medicine, and the nurse would apologize: no, narcotics could make certain conditions much worse, or complicate any needed surgery. "I'm not afraid of dying," Mom told her. "I'm afraid of *hurting*, but I'm not afraid of dying. My husband died nine years ago, and every night I tell God I'm ready to see him again."

Four days later, with no warning at all, she got her wish.

Stroke

Earth and air won't cease their quarrel. Tornadoes take up their form in the Midwest, a writhing cone of soil and breath and bite.

Hurricanes shoulder and churn off the Gulf Coast, each one a gray ferocity, a roaring violence of roiling water.

Volcanic ash rises in the Philippines. Air becomes mass; dust becomes rock; the sky is raining fire, and no hissing rain will come to cool it.

The ocean floor cracks open in the Pacific, heaving waves of nausea across the surface of the sea.

A scar down the middle of the Mississippi River unzips and fills the world with livid water.

In Nashville, a brain breaks open.

In the universe, a star folds in on itself.

And God said, *Let there be darkness.*

Dust to Dust

She left in a state much larger than herself—two fire trucks, an ambulance, a rolling stretcher pushed by big men. The neighbors waited in their doorways to see which of us would emerge on the stretcher. I texted my friend standing quietly across the street, one arm around her older daughter: "Mom fell. Maybe a stroke. Probably not too bad—she's still talking, and we'll be at the hospital in plenty of time."

Lights swirling, sirens wailing—that is how she left. She came back in a black box marked with her name and the day she died and the day they burned her body. Inside the box was a plastic bag of ashes, closed with a twist tie, like a loaf of bread.

Lexicon

NASHVILLE, 2012

Words my mother permitted me to say in childhood:
Damn.
Shit.
Fuck.
Piss.
Hell.

━

Words my mother did not permit me to say in childhood:
Snot.

━

The last words of my father's favorite joke:
Oh, shit. I stepped in the dog doo-doo.

━

The first words of my father's favorite poem:
It was Saturday evening,
The guests were all leaving,
O'Malley was closing the bar,
When he turned and he said
To the lady in red,
"Get out; you can't stay where you are."

━

The last words my mother ever spoke:

    Thank you.

—

The last words my father ever spoke:

    Stop it.

—

The words I spoke in the rooms where my parents were dying:

    I love you.
    It's OK.
    Don't worry.
    It's OK.
    I love you.

—

The words I couldn't say in the rooms where my parents were dying:

    Damn. Shit. Fuck. Piss. Oh, hell.

Drought

"Nothing is plumb, level, or square," Alan Dugan writes in "Love Song: I and Thou," a meditation on the persecutions of marriage. My own marriage is full of joy, but all day long I walk through this drought-plagued landscape thinking that nothing in the world is plumb, level, or square. Inside, wooden doors hang crooked in their frames; the hot wind blows them open. Outside, the land has tightened and contracted. To the east, forests are on fire.

The earth is cracked, constricted, a bloodless sore. Leaves that should be a hundred different colors are dusty and faded. In the garden, the soil is powder; brown stems lift from it as though they'd never had roots, as though they were formed by heat and air.

For months the land has been pulling away from the edges of the world. A day of rain weeks ago was not enough—hardly more than spit from a parched mouth. Nothing fills the cracks in the dry ground; nothing rises from the roots to hold up a flower.

Everyone is talking about the drought; everyone is worried, even in this town with a deep river running through it and all the water we can pay for only a twist of the faucet away. Every morning I drag the hose out and fill the birdbath with water. The desperate robins hardly wait for me to turn away before they crowd the edges of the shallow dish to drink and drink and drink.

WARBLER

Insomnia

A ll her tricks have failed, all the gentle seductions: the warm bath, the quiet book, the perfect sex, the cool sheets on the cool side of the bed, even the first unpanicked Benadryl and then the desperate second. She surrenders to it now, hoping only to live with it in peace, side by side, like an animal she has invited into the yard never expecting to tame. After a lifetime spent conjoined with sleep like a twin, like the truest friend, she is bereft, abandoned. So many hours in the night! She had no idea.

She will not think of the unworried man, the rebuke of his tranquil sleeping, or of their children, grown now, the ones who first taught her how to sleep lightly, tuned to the slightest infant sound. She will not think of her parents, who welcomed her between them after dreams she was too young to know were dreams. She will not think of how she misunderstood her mother's last fall, how she felt so sure it was a simple accident, a broken hip, perhaps a little stroke, wholly reversible in that early window after the ambulance arrived. She will not think of the way she sat in the front seat of the ambulance, obedient, when she ought to have insisted on a place in the back, a place where she could hold a still but still-warm hand.

She will not think of the troubles of the ones she loves, or of her own troubles. The night is long, but the days are rushing by, gone gone surely gone, and she thinks to remember what she might otherwise forget except for the gift of this endless night. She lists to herself the names of flowers that will bring butterflies to her yard next spring, and she tries to name the New World warblers, thirty-seven in all, that rest in her honeysuckle tangles on their migratory journey, and she considers the miracle that happens when afternoon light in summer becomes the afternoon light of early fall.

At last, somewhere between the magnolia warbler and the Tennessee, she feels in the back of her neck the click that sometimes signals the first moving gear in the great machine of sleep, and she turns on her side and settles the covers, just in case.

How to Make a Birthday Cake

Remember that one of your children won't eat buttercream icing and one won't eat cream cheese icing and one will eat only the layers and leave every morsel of icing absolutely untouched, a giant F-shaped slice of butter and cream. On his plate it's the Second Coming, but only the cake is raptured, leaving behind a skeleton of powdered sugar sin.

The no-icing kid prefers the brown sugar pound cake, remember, not the cream cheese pound cake or the sour cream pound cake. Remember that your grandmother's recipe for brown sugar pound cake is on a card labeled "Caramel Pound Cake" though there is not a hint of caramel in it. Remember how your grandmother always said "caramel" as though it rhymed with "carousel." Remember when your grandmother's handwriting was sure and strong and she could still see to copy out a receipt, as she sometimes called it, and remember when she was too weak and blind to bake but still knew the receipt for care-a-mel cake by heart.

Remember that the card is tucked into your mother's recipe box between the card for cranberry Jell-O mold and the card for brandied fruit. Wonder for the first time why she filed a cake recipe between two fruit recipes (or, really, two "fruit" recipes) until it finally comes to you: this must be the Thanksgiving section of the recipe box. There was always some taxonomy behind your mother's inscrutable systems, and her brown sugar pound cake recipe would of course be grouped with the squash soufflé and the pecan pie, too, because it goes without saying that there will be no pumpkin pie recipe in any Thanksgiving file created by your mother, who spent her childhood harvesting pecans in Lower Alabama.

When you pull out the eggs and the butter and the flour—plain, not self-rising; you will never make that mistake again—and the absurd quantities of sugar, remember to set the recipe card in a safe place. There are things you cannot keep safe, that you have already failed forever to keep safe, but you must remember to protect this one card written in your grandmother's hand and saved in your mother's recipe box. There's a child in your house who won't eat icing, and today is his birthday, and he will not always be a child, and you will not always keep him safe.

Homeward Bound

Every time my mother went to visit my sister or my brother, she would leave her brown dachshund with me. And for days afterward, the dog would sit before our back door and wait for her. This was the same door my mother used every night when she and the dog came over for supper, and its full-length window is the only one in our house that reaches low enough for a dachshund to see through. The dog would wait and wait and wait, and three days later—a week at most—my mother always came back to her.

Two weeks after Mom's funeral, the dog ran away. Dapple-colored, she was both willful and invisible: she had never once come when called, and she could disappear beneath the lowest bushes, behind the smallest fallen branch. Terrified, I turned that yard inside out looking for her. When I finally thought to check at my mother's house across the street, I found her at the back door, jumping up and scratching to be let in. She had been scratching so urgently, and for so long, that the paint was chipped away from the doorjamb.

What I Saved

I saved only one of your thirty-seven coffee mugs, the white one from the church in Birmingham with the massive pietà hanging behind the altar. I keep it in the back corner of the cupboard, next to the mug emblazoned with a troubling Bible verse that gets used only when all the other mugs are dirty.

I saved the nicest of the towels filling two closets but none of the fabric remnants piled in the guest room, and none of the garish rhinestone brooches from the fifties, and none of the Jane Austen fan fiction, and none of the *Southern Living* magazines from the eighties, and none of the Hallmark Channel DVDs. The retirement home, the one you almost moved into, was grateful to have the DVDs. The retirement home, you would be glad to know, has finally gotten rid of the bedbugs.

I saved all five giant boxes of OxiClean, and oh my God why did you never tell me about OxiClean? At 156 loads per box, our socks have been white for all the years you've been gone.

I saved three lipsticks in a shade of pink I will never wear, but I threw away two dozen more, along with bottle after bottle of expired vitamins, and don't even get me started on the expired boxes and cans in the pantry. I wish I had known how much you loved blueberry muffins. I wish I had made you blueberry muffins every day of your life.

I saved miles and miles of Christmas ribbon and boxes of note cards. Even after the funeral thank-you notes, there were enough cards left for all my correspondence for years to come.

I saved your nice wooden coat hangers, and I wish I'd saved the gorgeous red raincoat that was too big for me when you died but would fit perfectly now.

Naturally I saved the baptismal gown with the handmade lace and the impossibly dainty white-on-white embroidery, half a century old by the time I found it in your sock drawer, and I saved the socks, too, or at least the ones with mates.

I saved all the photos and all the love letters, and the recipe cards that can be dated, like ancient trees, by layers of butter stains. I saved your wedding ring and the pearl pendant with the diamond chip that Dad gave you, promising a lifetime of diamonds and pearls, though there was never any money for diamonds or pearls. I saved what was left of your wedding gown and the gown you wore on your wedding night. I saved Aunt Fidelis's silver vanity set with mermaids embossed on the Victorian hair receiver. Before I threw away your brush, I saved your snow-white hair, too. The pale, thin strands are almost invisible in the cut-glass jar where the mermaids keep watch.

I saved the empty bird feeders and the empty pots in the garage and even the nearly dead holly fern you dug up from our old yard and carried here in a plastic bag but didn't live to plant. I filled the feeders with seeds, and I filled the pots with flowers, and I planted the dry roots of the holly fern, and now my yard is filled with birds and blossoms. I saved all these things. But what I couldn't save weighs on my heart like a stone.

When My Mother Returns to Me in Dreams

NASHVILLE, 2012

I had wanted the story to be a gift, a tribute to the house my mother loved long past the time when love could save it. Mom was still refusing to leave, and I struggled to understand her fondness for a place that was tumbling into ruins around her. But as I was writing the essay, I began to grasp her deep-rooted reasons for staying, and why my arguments carried no weight against them. In trying to fathom my mother's love for that house, I came around to remembering my love for it, too. That would be my gift to her: understanding. The story was set to appear in a magazine my mother often read, and it would be illustrated with pictures of the house and our family's life in it—a photo of me in my First Communion gown, a picture of Mom in her wedding dress—and I planned to wrap up a copy for Mother's Day.

But my brother had his doubts: "It might make her feel bad for strangers to read about how terrible the house looks," he said. "She might be embarrassed." So I never said a word.

By the time the essay finally appeared in print, Mom had moved to Nashville, but it was months before she ever saw it. One day she banged open the door of my office and slammed a copy of the magazine down on the desk. "What is *this*?" she yelled, her face so flushed the scalp showed pink beneath her clean white hair.

I could see how it had happened. She sits down beneath the dryer at the beauty shop to flip through an old magazine. Suddenly she comes to a full-page picture from her own wedding album. There she is, standing with Dad on the church steps, squinting into the Lower Alabama sun, in the dress she'd designed and made by hand.

"Mom, listen," I started.

"No, *you* listen. What made you think it was OK to publish my picture in a magazine without even *asking* me?"

"I wanted it to be a surprise," I said. "I was planning to wrap it up for Mother's Day, but Billy thought it might hurt your feelings to read about how bad the house looks."

The air whooshed out of her. "Oh," she said. "Oh." She picked up the magazine and looked at the picture again. "Well, that's OK, then."

When Mom returns to me in dreams, she's always heartbreakingly herself, not some otherworldly haint or visible expression of my own grief. Whenever she appears, my first reaction is always relief. *Oh, thank God. It was just a misunderstanding. You're alive.* And Mom is always puzzled, always surprised when I grab her and hold her tight, when I say again and again, "You're here. You're back. Thank God."

And when I find her somewhere else, in an unfamiliar dream landscape, it's always somehow recognizably ordinary—not paradise at all but a cinder-block house with knotty-pine paneling and worn floral curtains. I walked into a strange house once and found Mom sitting with my father and my grandparents, and my father's godmother, and they all looked up when I opened the door, but they were no gladder to see me than if I had merely stepped outside to check the weather. My dead don't seem to know they're dead.

In one dream Mom was annoyed to discover her coat hangers in the closet next to our front door. "But why would you take *all* my nice wooden hangers?" she said.

"Because you died, Mom," I said. "You were dead."

"Oh," she said. "That's OK, then."

CICADA

Carapace

Hush. Be quiet. The long summer day is coming to a close, spooling up its lovely light, but there is nothing to fear from the night. There is nothing to fear from life giving way to death, for that matter, or from any dark thing. Stand in the shadows under the trees for only a moment, for half a moment, and a dozen fallen things will reveal themselves to you.

Last year's sassafras leaf, clinging still to a bit of its yellow luster, has gone gorgeous in lace, and the cicada, dwelling in the black soil for all those years, has climbed out of its shell and taken to the trees and begun to sing, has become the song of summer evenings, and the sweet-gum ball has lost its spiky armor and released its seeds into the generations, and the acorn, too, has shed its shell and sent roots into the earth, and the dead sycamore at the edge of the quiet lake's lapping water has leapt into flame as it does every single evening, and then the red-winged blackbird, the bright badge on his wing a flare of incandescence in the light at the end of the day, settles on a branch and sings the nighttime home.

Resurrection

A dozen monarch caterpillars arrive in the mail, tender, unprotected, but I am ready. I've set out an entire flat of native milkweed plants, new additions to a bed I planted earlier but that so far has not attracted a single breeding pair. I've enclosed the butterfly garden with a sturdy wire border covered by mosquito netting, to protect the caterpillars from birds and spiders and wasps and parasitic flies and praying mantises and the hundred other predators waiting outside. Even inside the enclosure, all manner of calamity could befall them: various diseases, poorly timed shifts in the weather, hungry animals with claws or beaks too sharp for mosquito netting to repel.

Within a day, sure enough, some other living thing has unfastened the netting from where I've pinned it tightly to the soil, pushed past it, and gulped down two of the caterpillars. Monarch larvae subsist entirely on poisonous milkweed leaves and are therefore toxic themselves, but they are not toxic enough to prevent all predation. A hungry bird will devour almost any insect, no matter how distasteful. My husband once plucked a large stinkbug from the driveway and tossed it out of harm's way. The instant it took to the air, a robin swept out of a tree and caught it mid-flight. This is a predator-friendly yard: I have set up nine feeding stations to welcome birds, and never mind the opossums and the raccoons and the rat snake that winters under the garden shed.

A day later, another two or three or four are gone, though their enclosure appears intact this time. Exactly how many are missing I am no longer sure, for despite their jaunty yellow and black stripes, monarch caterpillars are surprisingly good at hiding and instinctively freeze as soon as they see me approach. Possibly they are somewhere else in the garden altogether, for now I find a flaw in my rigged-together enclosure: the netting is not so tightly fastened to the ground as I had thought. A few old bricks solve that problem, but already I am waiting for the next problem to arise.

Very few caterpillars survive to become butterflies—perhaps as few as 1 percent—and nature responds with profligacy: a female monarch lays around four hundred eggs during her brief reproductive life. Before the widespread use of herbicides, this reproduction rate was enough to keep North America dense with butterflies. Now the monarchs are dying out, and I am invested in trying to save them.

How literally am I invested? I try not to count up the costs for milkweed, fencing, mosquito nets, the caterpillars themselves. But I find myself doing the math each time a caterpillar goes missing, recalculating what I will end up having paid for each monarch that ultimately survives. I know I am fast approaching the butterfly equivalent of what my country friend calls the forty-dollar homegrown tomato.

For a while—an hour, two—all seems well, but when I check again, a caterpillar has crawled onto the net and stopped moving. I'm not worried at first, and I'm only slightly worried a few hours later, but by morning something seems terribly wrong: for at least seventeen hours, this caterpillar has not moved at all, and creatures who eat for twenty-four hours each day should not remain so wholly still.

When I check again, for now I am checking obsessively, a black blob extends from its hind end, a sticky film of some kind, too large to be excrement. I think of the pet rabbit who died in my arms in childhood, how it gave a single kick and then fell limp, filling my lap with urine. Is this the way a monarch caterpillar surrenders its life, hanging upside down and spooling out a thread of thick black tar?

It's useless to return to my desk—there's no way I'll be able to work. I squat and wait. The internet urges monarch stewards to remove diseased caterpillars from their enclosures, but how can I be sure I know life from death in the odd demiworld of this garden, this mesh-enclosed anteway I have fashioned between the mailbox and the sky?

The caterpillar stirs, and finally I see: this is not a death at all but only a pause before another stage of life, splitting the skin it has outgrown and crawling away from what it no longer needs. It is a new creature. Even before it begins again, it begins again.

In Darkness

Early autumn is the heyday of the orb weaver spiders. A spider's egg sac bursts open in spring, and the infinitesimal hatchlings spend all summer growing and hiding from predators. By fall, they are large enough to emerge from their secret places and spin their marvelous webs. Every night the female makes an intricate trap for flying insects, and every evening she eats up the tatters of last night's web before starting in again on something new and perfect.

By September, our house always looks as though nature has decorated early for Halloween, but I can't bring myself to sweep the webs from the windows or out from under the eaves. I know the spiders are there, the few who survived the long, hot summer. They are crouched in corners, waiting for nightfall, when they will again commence to wring a miracle from the world. For beauty, what tidy window ever matched a spider's web glistening in the lamplight?

One year I watched an orb weaver spider at uncommonly close range. She had set up housekeeping by stringing her web from our basketball backboard to the corner of the house. Just above the eave on that corner is a floodlight that's triggered by motion. Every night that September I carried my late mother's lame old dachshund out for her last sniff around, and every night the light blinked on, catching the spider mid-miracle. While the ancient dog did her business, I stood in the shadows just beyond the reach of the light and watched the spider carrying on her urgent work. If I held still enough, she would keep spinning, and I could watch something unfold that normally takes place entirely in the dark. But whenever she saw me studying her, she would rush up the lifeline she'd spun for herself and squat behind the Christmas lights that dangle from the eaves, the ones that wink all day and warn birds who might otherwise crash into the windows when the slant of light changes in autumn.

Human beings are creatures made for joy. Against all evidence, we tell ourselves that grief and loneliness and despair are tragedies, unwelcome variations from the pleasure and calm and safety that in the right way of the world would form the firm ground of our being. In the fairy tale we tell ourselves, darkness holds nothing resembling a gift.

What we feel always contains its own truth, but it is not the only truth, and darkness almost always harbors some bit of goodness tucked out of sight, waiting for an unexpected light to shine, to reveal it in its deepest hiding place.

No Exit

"Marry an orphan," my mother used to say, "and you can always come home for Christmas." What she should have said: "Marry an orphan, or you'll have *four* parents to nurse through every torment life doles out on the long, long path to the grave." But I married the opposite of an orphan— the son and grandson of people who live deep into old age despite diseases that commonly fell others: cancer, sepsis, heart failure, emphysema, you name it. My husband's elders get sick, and then they get sicker, but for years they persevere.

My own father died of cancer five days shy of his seventy-fifth birthday. Mom dropped dead of a hemorrhagic stroke at eighty. When I checked on her the night before her death, she was eating a cookie and watching a rerun of *JAG*. I almost pointed out that eating in bed is a choking hazard, but for once I let it go. She was in good health, but she needed my help in countless annoying ways—annoying to her and annoying to me—and she was heartily sick of being told what to do. I take some comfort now in knowing I skipped that one last chance to boss her around.

There's an art to helping people without making them feel bad about needing help. It's an art I was learning but hadn't wholly mastered with Mom. "I would've died if my mother had done this to me when I was your age," she said when she moved in across the street, but by the time she actually died three years later, we had both adjusted: "I know I can be a bitch sometimes, but you can be a bitch sometimes too," she would say. "I figure it all works out in the wash."

I saw my mother at least twice a day and talked with her more often than that. But as close as we were, I sometimes found myself despairing her long-lived genes. My great-grandmother lived to be ninety-six despite spending the bulk of her life without antibiotics or vaccines. My grandmother lived to be ninety-seven despite being shot in her seventies by a crazed stranger. I knew my kids would one day leave for lives of their own, but Mom's needs would just keep growing. By the time my nest was truly empty, I thought, there would be precious little left of me.

When she died so suddenly, still issuing hilarious pronouncements and taking our teenagers' side in generational disputes, I felt as if a madman had blown a hole through my own heart. Unmoored, I could not stop weeping. Caring for elders is like parenting toddlers—there's a scan running in the background of every thought and every act, a scan that's tuned to possible trouble. And there's no way to shut it down when the worst trouble, irrecoverable trouble, comes.

A year later, before we'd even settled the question of where Mom's keepsakes should go, my husband's parents moved across several state lines to an assisted-living facility five minutes from our house. Physically frail—he from heart failure, she from Parkinson's disease—they needed far more help than my mother ever did, but I figured their new living arrangements would surely make up the difference. After cooking for Mom, driving her to appointments, managing her medications, paying her bills, and washing her clothes, I looked forward to having parents nearby who needed only our love and our company.

Years earlier, when we told people Mom was moving to Nashville, men would look at my husband incredulously: "You let your mother-in-law move in *next door*?" After my in-laws arrived, my friends said much the same thing to me. But clichés have no place in this story: my husband loved my parents, and I loved his.

My mother-in-law was in every way a divergence from the stereotype: preternaturally patient, radiant with love, alert for ways to support and approve of her children, including those who had joined her family by marriage. Soon after our wedding, I heard my husband griping in the next room about how much money I spent on toiletries. "I just don't see how anyone can drop thirty dollars in a drugstore without buying a single drug," he said. And I was astonished to hear my deeply traditional mother-in-law take my side: "Son, Margaret works hard. If she wants to take her money and stamp it into the mud, you can't say a thing about it."

So when my in-laws moved to Nashville, only my sister's objection struck home with me: "But you know how all this will end."

In fact, my father-in-law collapsed three days after arriving and had to be hospitalized, and the stress of the move dramatically worsened my mother-in-law's Parkinson's symptoms. One crisis followed another: infections, head injuries, broken bones, even a fire. And each disaster meant the need for more help from us, plus a constant stream of houseguests as my husband's far-flung siblings put their own lives on hold to pitch in. Back on the caregiving roller coaster, I struggled to remember the lesson I had just learned so painfully with Mom: the end of caregiving isn't freedom. The end of caregiving is grief.

Even as he recovered from open-heart surgery himself, my father-in-law continued to coordinate my mother-in-law's care. Once, overwhelmed by those responsibilities, he reminded my husband that in the old days families took their elders in. My husband reminded his father that in the old days people with heart failure and Parkinson's disease didn't live long enough to need the kind of help they already needed, never mind the inevitable disasters the future would bring.

My own mother could not afford assisted living, and we always understood that one day she would move in with us. But Mom wanted to be independent for as long as possible, and I had my own reasons for keeping at least a lawn between us: I work from a home office, and it would be nearly impossible to conduct my professional life with a needy elder in the very next room. The dilemma never had to be resolved with Mom, but it came up again once my mother-in-law entered hospice care. It broke my heart to imagine my beloved father-in-law living alone in that assisted-living facility after sixty years of happy marriage.

"But your dad would be lonely here too," I said to my husband. "If he moves in with us, I'd have to rent an apartment. Wouldn't it be better if he stayed in assisted living, where there are people around all day, and came over here for supper every night the way Mom did?"

My husband looked at me. "You mean an *office*, right?" he finally said. "If Dad moves in, you'd need to rent an office?"

I laughed. I meant an office, but for a moment he wasn't absolutely sure. And in the end, my father-in-law stayed put.

Of course, my father-in-law had a point: families once worked in a very different way. During the Depression, when my mother's childhood house burned to the ground, her whole family moved in with my great-grandparents. A few years later, my other great-grandmother moved in too. I was in college myself before the last of that generation passed away. "I've been taking care of people my whole life," my grandmother wondered. "What will I do with myself now?" As my mother-in-law entered the last stage of a savage disease, when just getting through the days was a dreadful challenge for her and for all of us who loved her, I constantly reminded myself of my grandmother's plaintive question.

Then we lost my beautiful mother-in-law too. I think of her, and of my parents, every single day. They are an absence made palpably present, as though their most vivid traits—my father's unshakable optimism, my mother's irreverent wit, my mother-in-law's profound gentleness—had formed a thin membrane between me and the world: because they are gone, I see everything differently.

No Such Thing as a Clean Getaway

One great-uncle fell from a third-floor window, possibly pushed by his wife. Another fell asleep before an unscreened fire and was burned to a black crisp, sitting in his armchair. Still another succumbed to a gas leak while sitting on the toilet. Amazingly, he was not the only uncle to meet his end in the bathroom, but circumstances are less clear with the other: Was his early death brought on by a heart condition, long known, or did he simply fall in a drunken haze and hit his head, the trouble with drink also being long known? No way to say: these are not family stories that get passed down in precise detail.

I remember well the difficult great-aunt whose stroke left her with a scrambled vocabulary but no fewer demands. Unsure what might come out of her mouth, she compensated, attaching every attempt to communicate with a declarative prefix. Her order at the diner: "It's true I want crayons." Her request to go home: "It's true I got to pee."

And what to tell the children about their ancestor, tiny but severe, who entered her dotage so sublimely unaware of social constraints that she was banned from community meals for masturbating in the dining room? Or the beloved elders who pulled back at the very end, no longer loving in their last hours, no longer concerned in the least for those they would leave behind? "Stop it," said my mostly unconscious father when I adjusted the pillows that left his neck crooked at an awkward angle. "Don't do that," said my mother-in-law as I stroked her hand.

Oh, the lives we grieve in their going. Oh, the lives we grieve in their going on.

Ashes, Part Two

NASHVILLE, 2015

My father-in-law is poring over an image of the marker he has ordered for my mother-in-law's grave. It will be set over the shoebox-sized plot where her ashes were put to ground a month ago, her parents and her grandparents beside her. My father-in-law is not sure the spacing between the letters looks quite even. He is not sure the carved lettering is quite deep enough. He is not sure each word appears on the correct line—perhaps the dates should come last? My grieving father-in-law sits at our table and studies the image for a long time. He asks us each in turn to look at the photocopied page that came in the mail from a mortuary more than five hundred miles away. Do *we* think the lettering is right? It must be perfect. It is his job to see that it's perfect. In time, his own marker will stand beside hers, and he will not be here to set it right.

He looks at me: "Where are Bill and Olivia buried?" He has never thought to ask before, though my mother has been gone for more than two years, my father for more than a decade.

My husband coughs and turns away. Our sons look at me.

"We haven't buried them yet," I say.

My father-in-law looks startled: "Where are they then?"

A sound that isn't strictly a cough erupts from my husband. I look at the boys.

"They're in Dad's closet," one of them tells his grandfather.

MAPLE

Nevermore

The rains we've been waiting for, yearning for, have finally arrived in our part of Tennessee, and the maple leaves are falling now in great clots. Rain is falling and leaves are falling and my youngest son, like his brothers, has received his selective service card in the mail, and today I have returned to my house to find a lone black vulture standing in my front yard.

I am always grateful to vultures, that indefatigable cleanup crew doing such necessary work along the roadsides. Nevertheless, a vulture adopting an attitude of possession toward my own home does not exactly constitute a welcome autumn tableau, especially not during a melancholy week of rain in the window and inescapable images of war licking at the edges of a mother's mind.

We live on an unkempt lot in a neighborhood where most of the lawns are pristine, and vultures are not common visitors. Yet here is one standing a few feet from my front door. I idle in the driveway to watch. It is eating nothing. It is only standing there, looking at my house. Occasionally it dips its head and hunches, mantling its wings, but there appears to be nothing at its feet, no prey to protect from encroachers. Nor any encroachers, for that matter.

I drive around back, walk through the house, open the front door. The vulture turns its bald, black face to look at me in that peculiar side-eyed way of birds, and then it flaps heavily off, low across the yard and up and over the house where my mother lived. When I let our old dog out, he sniffs again and again at the spot where the vulture was standing but comes to no discernible conclusions.

There is a newly dead chipmunk in the street, seemingly unnoticed by the vulture. I think it must surely have registered the dead chipmunk's existence at some visceral level; surely the dead chipmunk is what has summoned this bird to my yard. The chipmunk has been a sort of housemate of mine, living in an elaborate tunnel system under our foundation, and I don't like to think of it lying unmourned in the rain-soaked street. I step back from the doorway and wait, hoping the vulture will come and claim its prize.

But these are willed thoughts, a hedge against an atavistic instinct to read omens and signs into a giant black vulture that has staked out my home on a day when the federal government has announced its intention to claim my child. I think of myself as a rational person. I am not a reader of portents or horoscopes. I greet the promises of fortune cookies with wry hope at best, but there was a time, more than two decades ago, when I hand-delivered twenty copies of a chain letter on the last day before bad luck was supposed to descend on anyone who dared to break the chain. I was not in my right mind: I had recently suffered two devastating miscarriages and was precariously pregnant again with a child that no one expected to live. I stuck a bunch of chain letters in the mailboxes of people I did not know, just to be safe.

That child registered for the selective service two years ago, and now it is his younger brother's turn. If a simple card in the mail can cast me back into the ancient reach of augury, I can only imagine the dread that claws at the heart of a mother whose child is serving in a part of the world where dangers are real and not merely imagined—where fear is of a piece with sacrifice and not of superstition.

I know a vulture is only a bird, only a bird and not an omen, no matter the temptation to turn it into the equivalent of Poe's raven. Arriving shrouded in widow's weeds and standing in solitary magnificence to stare at me with one unblinking eye, it is still only a bird, a big, black bird entirely indifferent to the workings of the human realm. Unaware of the workings of the human heart.

When I leave to walk the old dog after dark, the unlucky chipmunk is still lying in the road where it met its end. The next morning I wake up late. When I finally sit down at my desk and look out the window, there's not one trace of the former chipmunk clinging to the asphalt, not one glossy black feather resting on the grass.

History

"Your hand feels just like your mother's hand," my father tells me as we walk hand in hand. I am twelve. I pull my hand back, hold it out before me: dirty fingernails, torn cuticles, no ring. It is not my mother's hand. It is nothing like my mother's hand. It is only my hand.

—

Mom finishes hemming the confirmation dress while I'm at school. The dress has two hems, really—one for the yellow foundation, and one for the gauzy filament of see-through daisies that floats on top. When I try it on, it is just barely too long. It touches the floor, and the daisies are too fragile to be dragged across the asphalt parking lot—the gauze will be rags by the time I'm called to the altar. There's no time to rip out the hems, pin them up again, and make all those tiny stitches, so close together they can't be kicked out by an eighth-grader walking in a floor-length dress. "Wear these," Mom says. My first heels, all of one inch high. My feet settle into the slight indentations my mother's heels have made, where the balls of my mother's feet bend, where my mother's toes spread out. The shoes fit perfectly.

—

The wedding gown has spent twenty-eight years in an Alabama attic. "There's bound to be nothing left of it," I say. What dry rot hasn't ruined, the moths have surely long since eaten.

"We'll see," my mother says, kneeling beside the bathroom tub, squeezing baby shampoo through the stained Chantilly lace she sewed seed pearls into so many years before, through the shot silk she ordered from England for the gown she'd designed herself. Half a dozen soakings in the tub, half a dozen mornings spread out on a sheet in a sunny backyard, and the dress is white again. Days more with the finest-gauge thread, a magnifying glass hanging from a chain above patient fingers, and the torn bits are whole once more, the scallops at the collarbone perfectly rounded, the points at the wrists exactly centered. I step into its white tumult, slip my hands through a filigree of sleeves, and hold my breath while she zips. Not a single seam needs adjustment.

＿

My mother had three children between thirty and thirty-six, and I had three children between thirty and thirty-six. Now my body is an exact replica of her own. I see her in my own thickening waist. I watch as her feet propel me through the world. I feel her in the folds of my neck and the set of my brow and the slight curve of the finger where I wear the ring my father gave her. The ring she never took off but had to leave behind.

Ashes, Part Three

LOWER ALABAMA, 2017

After her own death, I suddenly understood Mom's reluctance to consign Dad to the ground. At first it was just impossible; there was no way to drive so far, from Nashville to Lower Alabama, through streaming tears. Later, the logistics were daunting: How would we get permission to open the family plot by even a posthole digger's width when it was already accommodating as many of our dead as it could officially hold? We all agreed that driving in at midnight was out of the question: this was the deepest part of rural Alabama, where everyone is armed. Permission from the preacher would be required.

On the fifth anniversary of Mom's death, it came.

⟷

I am dreaming when the alarm goes off the morning my siblings and I leave to take our mother's ashes home. In the dream, some children and I are singing: "Ashes, ashes, we all fall down." One child stops the game and says severely, "We aren't supposed to have ashes in our pockets."

⟷

On I-65, just past Prattville, kudzu smothers every fencerow, and I strain to see the famous mill wheel, no longer turning, through the tangle of vines, but the GO TO CHURCH OR THE DEVIL WILL GET YOU sign is gone now. We turn off the interstate after Montgomery onto the blue highway that will take us home, to the place I still think of as home though I have not been there in years, not since my grandmother's death. The mimosas are in bloom. In the pastures that spread back from the road, egrets stand upon the dozing cows and pick at the edges of the ponds near the road.

We pass the last house our grandparents lived in—the one they built from cinder blocks when the big house became too much for them to keep up—and head straight for the church. In its cemetery, a mockingbird sings in a tree by the gate, competing with another mockingbird in the pines across the yard. Birdsong and wind are the only sounds in this corner of the universe.

My brother takes out the posthole digger, which I packed primarily as a symbol, a nod to the specificity of Mom's plan. I did not expect it to be useful, at least not compared to the long-blade shovel I also packed. But the posthole digger, it turns out, is the perfect tool. Decades after she left her birthplace for good, our mother still remembered the exact texture of its soil, a mixture made mostly of red sand and dust that yields to the blades with no resistance at all. Within only a minute or two, my brother has dug a hole large enough to hold our parents' ashes.

He opens the boxes, and then the boxes within the boxes, and then the plastic bags within those, and he shakes the ashes into the hole. It would be easy to scrape the leftover soil into the hole with only our feet, but we all seem to have a vague, unspoken sense that kicking dirt into a grave would be disrespectful, though neither of our parents had been the sort to stand on ceremony. My brother and sister and I each take up a handful of dirt to drop into the hole on top of the ashes. We look at each other. Should we sing? Say a few words of prayer? No one steps forward to lead, and so my brother finishes up with the shovel. The mockingbirds sing their own hymns, and we all step on the mounded dirt to pack the soil tight.

They are buried now in the graveyard between the church where Mom was baptized and the schoolhouse where she learned to read. They are buried now deep in the soil she sprang from, deep in the soil her parents sprang from, deep in the soil their parents sprang from. They are buried near all those who came before them, too far back for anyone to remember.

Masked

When they first appeared in the neighborhood, I assumed they were starlings. A flock of starlings is the bane of the bird feeder—a vast, clamoring mob of unmusical birds soiling the windshields and lawn furniture, muscling one another aside so violently that no other birds dare draw near the suet.

But this flock stayed high in the treetops, far from my feeders, too far away to recognize. Then a cold snap kept all the puddles frozen for days, and every bird in the zip code showed up at my heated birdbath to drink. That's how I finally got close enough to know them for what they were: cedar waxwings, the most exotic of all the backyard birds. They are here in Middle Tennessee only during late fall and winter, when the hollies and hackberries and Japanese honeysuckle are bearing fruit. Seeing the entire flock at my birdbath seemed like a miracle.

But there's a new slant of light in winter, and the trees surrounding the house are bare now, casting no shade. For birds, this combination can be deadly. Our windows have turned into mirrors, giving back the sky and making a solid plane look like an opening. I've made every adjustment I can—installed screens, put stickers on the glass door, hung icicle lights from the rafters—but migratory birds can be especially vulnerable to disorientation near unfamiliar buildings. The day after the waxwings appeared at my birdbath, I found one of them, its flock long gone, panting on the driveway below a corner of the house where two windows meet and form a mirage of trees and distances. When I stooped to look at the bird, it lay there quietly.

Though I could see no sign of injury, I knew it must be grievously hurt to sit so still as I gently cupped my hands around it to move it to a safer place in the yard. It made a listless effort to peck at my thumb, but it didn't struggle at all when my fingers closed around its wings, and I didn't know what to do. So much beauty is not meant to be held in human hands.

Those golden breast feathers fading upward to pale brown, and backward to gray, give the cedar waxwing a kind of borrowed glow, as though it were lit at all times by sunlight glancing off snow. Its pointed crest and dashing mask—a wraparound slash of black—sharpen its pale watercolors into a mien of fierceness. It's a tiny bandit with flamboyant red wingtips and a brash streak of yellow across the end of its tail feathers. An operatic aria of a bird. A flying jungle flower. A weightless coalescence of air and light and animation. It was a gift to hold that lovely, dying creature in my hands. It was wrong to feel its death as a gift.

I didn't know it was dying. I knew but didn't know. At least half of all birds who fly into windows will ultimately die of internal bleeding, even when they seem to recover and fly away, and this stunned cedar waxwing was in no shape to fly. Even so, my only thought in that moment was to set it high in a tree where our dog couldn't kill it with a curious sniff.

In any crisis I always seem to find myself suspended between knowing and not knowing, between information and comprehension. When my middle son was a toddler, he hit his head and briefly stopped breathing. I had been trained in CPR, but knowing exactly how to position a small body for help, knowing exactly how gently to puff into a baby's lungs, didn't figure into a scene in which my own child was in danger. I snatched him up and cradled him while his lips turned gray and my husband called the ambulance. In a contest between knowledge and instinct, instinct wins every time.

I should have taken that injured bird someplace safe and warm to die. Instead I took it to a cypress tree a few feet away and set it on a limb deep in the greenery. Its feet worked spastically for purchase but finally caught hold. It was clinging to the branch when I left it to go back inside. By the time I returned fifteen minutes later, it had tumbled into the soft ground cover below. One wing was spread out like a taxidermist's display, those waxy red tips stretched as far apart as fingers in a reaching hand. I didn't need to pick it up to know it was dead. I knew it was dead, but I hadn't known it was dying.

Why didn't I know? My mother died of a cerebral hemorrhage, and I have seen up close what it looks like when a living thing is dying because its brain is bleeding and there's nowhere for the pooled blood to go, no way to keep the blood from crowding out the living cells of thought, the living cells of self. "I love you," I said as we waited for the results of my mother's CT scan. "You're my good mama," I told her as her eyes closed. "Thank you," she said. I was waiting for the doctor to come and tell me what to do, and I didn't know that these would be her last words. I knew but didn't know.

I wish I had taken that soft brown miracle of a bird into a dark, warm room to die. I wish I hadn't noticed the way my mother's hand was already cooling when she took her last breath.

You'll Never Know How Much I Love You

NASHVILLE, 2018

I don't know exactly where it came from—this phrase of pure treacle, worse than cliché. My father kept the car radio tuned to the big band station, the oldies channel of his middle age, so I could have heard the words in a song sung long before my time. Perhaps I heard it on the transistor radio I kept clutched to my ear the year I was ten or eleven, that age when language sticks, when poems and song lyrics and incantatory prayers merge with the rush of blood in the veins. Now, more than forty years later, the songs on my transistor radio are playing on the oldies channel of my own middle age. I will never learn the new doxology.

Possibly I read it in a terrible novel, or the cropped version of a terrible novel. In those days they came bound five or six to a volume from *Reader's Digest*, blessedly pruned books by authors who felt no uneasiness about writing a sentence like "You will never know how much I love you."

Did someone say it to me once? In the desperate madness of mismatched love, did a boy whisper those very words into my very ear, where they found a place to latch, lingering decades longer than a love that now seems hardly more than a dream?

No matter. Somehow it worked its way into the sinews of my thinking, into the folds of my always unfolding memory. I hear it in my sleep; it comes to me while I'm washing dishes or watering the garden, snakes around my ears and slithers into my hair, settling like an invisible crown, too tight, on my skull.

I was six when I lost my first love, a boy whose family stayed across the road and up the hill while my own family left town. *You will never know how much I love you because I am too young for such words, because I am too young to be the vessel of longing and fury that I have become.* Did I already know, even then? Was I already so tuned to loss that a single line of pure banality could lodge in the reptilian brain?

A woman I thought of as a friend once said to me, "Your central motivation is fear of loss." It was not a description but an accusation. She meant I was a coward. She meant I was destined to go nowhere, accomplish nothing. It occurred to me to wonder if she had ever, even once, loved anyone enough to fear the possibility of loss, but that thought was as ugly as her own, and in any case she was not wrong.

What makes a little girl walk into her parents' room in the middle of the night and lay her hand on each in turn, a touch too light to wake them, just to be sure they're still breathing? My hand rises and falls with each breath they take. I turn to leave. They will never know I've been there. They will never know how much I love them.

ROBIN

Separation Anxiety

NASHVILLE, 2018

It is dusk in August, and the voices of robins fill the air, sur-
rendering daylight with one last call-and-response song
against the darkness. All spring I watched these birds building
their nests and raising their nestlings, heard those sharp-eyed
babies making their harsh, monosyllabic demands. All summer I watched the parents teaching their fledglings to flutter
up from the ground and into the tree limbs, or at least the in-
ner branches of a dense shrub, as quickly as they could. Now
the young birds have grown past the one-note call of desper-
ation, and the robins are all, young and old, singing the same
song. At twilight it is a mournful sound—something less than
heartbreaking, something more than melancholy.

Or maybe this edging sadness has nothing to do with
robins. Summer is ending, and my younger sons—the only
two still at home even part of the year—are heading back to
college, and I can hardly bear to see them go. When my children were younger, the connection I felt to them was visceral.
During those early days of carrying a child—whether in my
body or in my arms—I came to feel like one-half of a symbiotic
relationship. All these years later, motherhood still thrums
within me like a pulse, and I catch myself swaying whenever
I'm standing in a long line, soothing the ghost baby fussing
in my arms. I look at my sons, all taller than six feet now, and
sometimes I can't quite believe I'm not still carrying them
around on my hip, not still feeling their damp fingers tangled
in my hair or clutching the back of my blouse. Sometimes at

supper, when one of them brings a glass to his lips, I can still imagine a sippy cup gripped in his fingers.

I haven't forgotten how exhausting it was to be the mother of young children or how often I was frustrated by the close rooms and constricted plans of those days, the way my boys were always in my arms or at my feet. I haven't forgotten how repetitive those days were, how I often felt unable to draw a deep breath.

And yet I sometimes let myself imagine what a gift it would be to start all over again with this man, with these children, to go back to the beginning and feel less restless this time, less eager to hurry my babies along. Why did I spend so much time watching for the next milestone when the next milestone never meant the freedom I expected? There will be years and years to sleep, I know now, but only the briefest weeks in which to smell a baby's neck as he nestles against my shoulder in the deepest night.

With my own nest emptying, metaphors of loss are everywhere. The limping old dog who was my sons' perfect childhood companion is gone now, and I take my after-supper walk alone. I watch the sun dropping behind my neighbors' houses, and I listen to the robins' song. It's too late in the day for most songbirds and too early for owls; the robins have the stage to themselves in this margin between light and dark. I listen with an edge of grief around my heart. Summer is going, and daylight is going, and now my children are on their way again as well.

Already they are packing the minivan we bought when the youngest was in second grade. The house that all summer has been loud with life will fall almost silent. My husband and I will drive them to their dorms on the other side of the state, take a few minutes to unload, and then turn around to head home again. I will lift a hand as we pull out, though I know they will already be turning away, turning toward their beckoning new life. It has been years since the last time they looked back after leaving a car. They long ago stopped waving goodbye.

Farewell

Again and again I have to teach myself the splendor of
decay. The cerulean feathers drifting beneath the pine
where the bluebird met the Cooper's hawk for the last time.
The muddle of spent spikes on the butterfly bush, winter-dried
to the palest rustle. The blighted rose, its tangled canes gone
black and monstrous in death, baring now the fine archi-
tecture of the cardinal's nest it sheltered last summer. The
gathered dust on the living room piano throwing off light like
sparks in the waning day, and the cut lilies' petals, released in
one long sigh.

Recompense

It's your birthday, which always seems to fall on the most splendid day of October. Even if it's a workday, you must find some time to set aside your whirring machines and your contentions. Maybe there is a creek that all summer was still and dry and now is wet and tumbling with twigs and leaves and sweetgum balls. Maybe there is a field gone golden with weeds, with finches perched in the seed crowns. Maybe there is an old train track that hosts no trains but lays out a whole parade route of purple thistles, or a dirt road where the close pines have set down a thick carpet for your hurting feet. Maybe there is a lake where a bald eagle sometimes fishes, where you might chance to see it dive, to hear its wings rise up to break its fall, to watch its yellow feet pull a sleek brown fish from the green water.

And while you are walking, keeping your eyes turned to the sky, maybe the earth will pull you back to the path, back to the toddler holding up her hands to the drifting leaves; and to the floating meadow of duckweed the color of new grass in springtime; and to the lone frog calling with no response from the marshy backwater; and to all the sunning turtles lined up on their black logs like rosary beads; and to the crows and the blue jays conducting a bitter dispute high in the treetops; and to the young woman with a prosthetic arm sitting on a bench and telling a story with wild gesticulations while her sweetheart gazes at her, smiling, never lifting his eyes from hers. And maybe you will see two vultures, as beautiful on the wing as any eagle, circling the sky, and all the while the leaves will be letting go of their branches and falling down on you like blessings.

MONARCH

Late Migration

Every monarch in North America is hatched on the leaf of a milkweed plant, and almost all of them spend winter on fir-covered mountains in central Mexico, in clumps so thick that tree branches can crash to the forest floor from their weight. One recent March, a storm brought such shattering winds and rain to their Mexican wintering grounds that millions of butterflies died before they could head north to breed. And the milkweed that the survivors were looking for—once ubiquitous on American roadsides and in vacant lots and at the stubbled edges of farms—is mostly gone now too, a casualty of the herbicides that go hand in glove with genetically modified crops.

Twenty years ago, there were at least a billion monarch butterflies in North America. Now there are only ninety-three million. Once upon a time, even a loss of that magnitude might have caused me only a flicker of concern, the kind of thing I trusted scientists to straighten out. But I am old enough now to have buried many of my loved ones, and loss is too often something I can do nothing about. So I lie awake in the dark and plot solutions to the problems of the pollinators—the collapse of the honeybee hives and the destruction of monarch habitats—in the age of Roundup.

When it was time to put my garden to bed one fall, I pulled out the okra and squash and tomatoes and planted a pollinator garden: coreopsis and coneflower and sage and lavender and bee balm and a host of other wildflowers. Once spring came, I threw in a handful of zinnia seeds to fill in when the perennials were bloomed out. The crowning glory of the garden that first year was a flat of native milkweed plants. I know this scruffy half-acre lot is no match for what ails the pollinators, especially not in suburbia, where lawn services dispense poisons from tanks the size of pickup trucks. Around here I think I might be the only one losing sleep over the bees and the butterflies.

Our feist mix, Betty, was always in intense pursuit of moles. In a spray of dirt like something from a Road Runner cartoon, she could dig up a mole run in a matter of minutes, leaving a system of open trenches crisscrossing the yard. Once the mole was dead or had taken refuge under the roadbed, I would rake the mounds of dirt smooth again, cover the turned soil with white clover, and water it down.

"Rye?" a neighbor asked, watching me scatter seeds.

"Clover," I said.

She looked at me. "You're *planting* clover?"

"For the honeybees," I said.

"Last summer there was a big ball of bees up in the crepe myrtle next to my garbage cans," she told me. "It took a whole can of Raid to kill them."

Spring brought a nice crop of clover that year and the first blooms in the butterfly garden. The native bumblebees loved the new flowers, crawling into them with a fervor that explains how they got all mixed up in a metaphor for sex in the first place. But I never saw more than one honeybee, and the monarchs apparently never noticed the milkweed plants with their rangy stalks full of vibrant orange flowers. Oh, there were other butterflies: cabbage whites and clouded sulfurs and Gulf fritillaries with their deceptive orange wings. But the milkweed bloomed and faded without a single monarch arriving in the nursery I had built for them.

There will be another summer, I told myself.

That fall, with temperatures still unseasonably warm for Middle Tennessee, I watered the butterfly garden through a profound drought that lasted for more than two months. Only the zinnias were still blooming, and I debated with myself the right way to approach the weeks of unexpected flowers. Cut the spent blooms back and force the plants to keep making new flowers for any butterflies still on the wing? Or let the zinnias go to seed for goldfinches to harvest?

As with most quandaries, I came to an inadvertent compromise: cutting the dead blooms when I thought to, ignoring them when I didn't. So the goldfinches had their zinnias, and the Gulf fritillaries had theirs, too.

And then, a miracle. Walking to the mailbox on a sunny November afternoon, I spied a flash of orange in the flower bed. I was a step or two on before I saw it: a monarch, riding a hot-pink zinnia nodding in the wind. I walked closer, and there on a yellow zinnia was another. And on the red one too—and on the orange, the white, the peach ones. Monarch after monarch after monarch was gathering nectar from the flowers. All that mild afternoon, my butterfly garden was a resting place for monarchs making a very late migration to Mexico.

Monarchs migrate as birds do, but it takes the monarch four generations, sometimes five, to complete the cycle each year: no single butterfly lives to make the full round-trip from Mexico to their northern breeding grounds and back. Entomologists don't yet understand what makes successive generations follow the same route their ancestors took, and I can only hope that the descendants of these monarchs will find respite in my garden, too. Every year will always find me planting zinnias, just in case.

After the Fall

This talk of making peace with it. Of feeling it and then finding a way through. Of closure. It's all nonsense.

Here is what no one told me about grief: you inhabit it like a skin. Everywhere you go, you wear grief under your clothes. Everything you see, you see through it, like a film.

It is not a hidden hair shirt of suffering. It is only you, the thing you are, the cells that cling to each other in your shape, the muscles that are doing your work in the world. And like your other skin, your other eyes, your other muscles, it too will change in time. It will change so slowly you won't even see it happening. No matter how you scrutinize it, no matter how you poke at it with a worried finger, you will not see it changing. Time claims you: your belly softens, your hair grays, the skin on the top of your hand goes loose as a grandmother's, and the skin of your grief, too, will loosen, soften, forgive your sharp edges, drape your hard bones.

You are waking into a new shape. You are waking into an old self.

What I mean is, time offers your old self a new shape.

What I mean is, you are the old, ungrieving you, and you are also the new, ruined you.

You are both, and you will always be both.

There is nothing to fear. There is nothing at all to fear. Walk out into the springtime, and look: the birds welcome you with a chorus. The flowers turn their faces to your face. The last of last year's leaves, still damp in the shadows, smell ripe and faintly of fall.

Holy, Holy, Holy

On the morning after my mother's sudden death, before I was up, someone brought a basket of muffins, good coffee beans, and a bottle of cream—real cream, unwhipped—left them at the back door, and tiptoed away. I couldn't eat. The smell of coffee turned my stomach, but my head was pounding from all the tears and all the what-ifs playing across my mind all night long, and I thought perhaps the cream would make a cup of coffee count as breakfast if I could keep it down.

When I poured just a drip of cream into my cup, it erupted into volcanic bubbles in a hot spring, unspooling skeins of bridal lace, fireworks over a dark ocean, stars streaking across the night sky above a silent prairie.

And that's how I learned the world would go on. An irreplaceable life had winked out in an instant, but outside my window the world was flaring up in celebration. Someone was hearing, "It's benign." Someone was saying, "It's a boy." Someone was throwing out her arms and crying, "Thank you! Thank you! Oh, thank you!"

So much to do still, all of it praise.

DEREK WALCOTT

Works Cited

Not all allusions in *Late Migrations* are cited in the text. Here is a list of those that aren't:

p. 2: The title is a paraphrase of "Nature, red in tooth and claw" from "In Memoriam" by Alfred, Lord Tennyson.

p. 9: The phrase "Life piled on life" appears in "Ulysses" by Alfred, Lord Tennyson.

p. 30: The final two sentences of "The Snow Moon" are an echo of "mon semblable,—mon frère!" from Charles Baudelaire's *Les Fleurs du mal*.

p. 45: *Barney Beagle Plays Baseball*, a beginning reader by Jean Bethell, was first published in 1963.

p. 51: "Operation Apache Snow" was a US offensive launched on May 10, 1969, against the North Vietnamese that resulted in massive casualties on both sides.

p. 54: The title is a quotation from the poem "Tell Me a Story" by Robert Penn Warren.

p. 58: In the first sentence, "heavy bored" is an allusion to "Dream Song 14" by John Berryman.

p. 58: The Bible passage that closes the first paragraph is Mark 11:23.

p. 69: The "Beatitudes" commonly refers to a set of teachings delivered by Jesus in the Sermon on the Mount.

p. 72: "Ev'ry Time We Say Goodbye" is a song written by Cole Porter and recorded by Ella Fitzgerald, among others.

p. 78: "The world is too much with us" is an allusion to William Wordsworth's sonnet of the same title.

p. 80: The title of this essay alludes to a line from W. H. Auden's poem "Musée des Beaux Arts."

p. 85: The description of my mother as someone who never prepared for gardening is an echo of E. B. White's description of his wife, Katharine S. White, in an introduction to her book, *Onward and Upward in the Garden*.

p. 95: Annie Dillard's essay is "Total Eclipse," first published in 1982.

p. 96: The song I mention in the penultimate paragraph of this essay is "Ring of Fire," written by June Carter and Merle Kilgore and made famous by Johnny Cash.

p. 98: The short story we read in class, I later learned, is "Brandenburg Concerto" by Lawrence Dorr.

p. 110: In the final paragraph, "goldengrove unleaving" is an allusion to "Spring and Fall," a poem by Gerard Manley Hopkins.

p. 114: "Shaking the caked red dirt from my sandals" is an echo of Matthew 10:14.

p. 116: The title of this essay is an allusion to a line from William Shakespeare's "Sonnet LXXIII."

p. 116: "Nothing gold can stay" is an allusion to Robert Frost's poem of the same title.

p. 118: "Heart of Greyhound darkness" is an allusion to Joseph Conrad's novel *Heart of Darkness*.

p. 129: "The fog comes on little cat feet" is an allusion to "Fog" by Carl Sandburg.

p. 131: The title refers to an observation commonly attributed to Aristotle.

p. 132: "Two by Two" refers to the way the animals entered Noah's ark in Genesis 7:9.

p. 138: The title of this essay quotes a line from W. H. Auden's poem, "Musée des Beaux Arts."

p. 151: "He Is Not Here" is a quote from the Biblical Easter story.

p. 159: "You Can't Go Home Again" echoes the title of a novel by Thomas Wolfe.

p. 163: The title of this essay echoes repeated exhortations throughout the Bible.

p. 166: "Dust to Dust" echoes Ecclesiastes 3:20.

p. 175: "Homeward Bound" echoes the title of a 1993 film about three family pets making their way home after an unexpected separation from their people.

p. 187: "No Exit" echoes the title of a play by Jean-Paul Sartre.

p. 195: "Nevermore" is the word the bird repeats throughout Edgar Allan Poe's poem "The Raven."

p. 219: "Holy, Holy, Holy," is the title of a Christian hymn published in 1826 by Reginald Heber.

A final note: "In Which My Grandmother Tells the Story of the Day She Was Shot" is an edited version of an essay my grandmother wrote in 1983 that was never published. All the other essays in her voice are transcripts of interviews my brother conducted with her in 1990. The excerpts are faithful to the original recordings except where slight changes—adding names, for example, or omitting repetition—contribute significantly to understanding.

Publications

These essays appeared, often in significantly different form, in the following publications:

"Separation Anxiety" (as "Motherhood and the Back-to-College Blues")
The New York Times, August 20, 2018

"Gall" (as "What to Expect")
O, The Oprah Magazine, October 2018

"Homeward Bound" (as "What It Means to Be Loved by a Dog")
The New York Times, June 18, 2018

"Howl" (as "The Pain of Loving Old Dogs")
The New York Times, February 25, 2018

"Babel" and "Thanksgiving" (as "It's Thanksgiving. Come On Home")
The New York Times, November 23, 2017

"A Ring of Fire" (as "In Nashville's Sky, a Ring of Fire")
The New York Times, August 21, 2017

"Holy, Holy, Holy"
River Teeth, July 27, 2017

"The Unpeaceable Kingdom" (as "Springtime's Not-So-Peaceable Kingdom")
The New York Times, June 4, 2017

"Masked" (as "What Dying Looks Like")
The New York Times, February 26, 2017

"Late Migration"
Guernica, December 6, 2016

"Nevermore" (as "Quoth the Vulture 'Nevermore'")
The New York Times, October 31, 2016

"Recompense"
Proximity, September 13, 2016

"Red in Beak and Claw"
The New York Times, July 31, 2016

"No Exit" (as "Caregiving: A Burden So Heavy, until It's Gone")
The New York Times, August 8, 2015

Acknowledgments

It takes a village to raise a child. It takes a multigenerational nation to publish a first book at the age of fifty-seven.

I am grateful to the writers who helped shape these essays from an embryonic stage: Ralph Bowden, Maria Browning, Susannah Felts, Carrington Fox, Faye Jones, Susan McDonald, Mary Laura Philpott, and Chris Scott. Extra thanks to Maria, who read the whole book—twice—while it was still trying to become a book.

I am unendingly thankful for the writers at *Chapter 16* and for the Tennessee authors, librarians, and independent booksellers whose work gives *Chapter 16* its mission. I will never find enough words of thanks for Serenity Gerbman and Tim Henderson at Humanities Tennessee. For ten years their flexibility and unflagging support made it possible for me to be both an editor and a writer.

At *The New York Times*, I'm profoundly grateful to Peter Catapano, whose genius makes my words better every single week, and to Clay Risen, whose offhand remark in a conversation at the Southern Festival of Books—"Would you ever want to write about that?"—led to the first essay I wrote for both the *Times* and this book.

Joey McGarvey plucked an incomplete manuscript of *Late Migrations* out of the slushpile at Milkweed Editions and somehow saw what it could become. Her gentle guidance and brilliant editing turned a jumble of essays into an actual book. And after it finally became a book, the rest of the team at Milkweed— Meagan Bachmayer, Jordan Bascom, Shannon Blackmer, Joanna Demkiewicz, Daley Farr, Allison Haberstroh, Daniel Slager, Mary Austin Speaker, Abby Travis, and Hans Weyandt— worked unceasingly to help it find its way. Thank you, all of you.

Writing *Late Migrations* has brought home to me how vast the literary ecosystem truly is. I send my heartfelt thanks to Kristyn Keene Benton of ICM Partners for her expansive understanding and expertise; to Carmen Toussaint of Rivendell Writers' Colony for building the haven where this book could grow; to Mary Grey James, who came out of retirement to help me understand the book business from a side I'd never seen before; and to Karen Hayes and everyone at Parnassus Books for creating a crucial "third place" for Nashville's readers and writers, and for believing in this book from the very beginning.

All my life I have been wholly fortunate in teachers and mentors, especially Ruth Brittin, James Dickey, John Egerton, Sharyn Gaston, Ann Granberry, and R.T. Smith. Most of them didn't live to read this book, but their influence can be found in every paragraph. Teachers everywhere, thank you. You are planting seeds for the ages.

In eighth grade, having exhibited no competence in middle school biology, I abandoned my plan to be a large-animal veterinarian. When I told my parents I'd decided to be a writer instead, they bought an ancient manual typewriter at a garage sale and brought it home. I wrote all my high school, college, and grad school papers on that Underwood Noiseless Portable, and probably a thousand poems, too. That's the kind of parents I had.

It's the kind of family I still have: part safety net and part trampoline. I am grateful to Shannon Weems Anderson and Max Weems III, the cousins who shared so much of my childhood. I am grateful to our Nashville family—the Hills, the Baileys, the Michaels, the Tarkingtons, and all the dear friends who make our entire neighborhood a home. I am grateful to my brilliant siblings, Billy Renkl and Lori Renkl, who are my constant inspiration. I am grateful to Sam Moxley, Henry

Moxley, and Joe Moxley, the greatest gifts of my life. Most of all, I am grateful to Haywood Moxley, who is life itself to me.

In the end, this book is for my people. For my parents and my grandparents and my great-grandparents. For my husband and our children and, someday, for the families our children will make. For my brother and my sister. For my husband's parents and siblings. For all our beloved nieces and nephews on both sides. If there's anything that living in a family has taught me, it's that we belong to one another. Outward and outward and outward, in ripples that extend in either direction, we belong to one another. And also to this green and gorgeous world.

Heidi Ross

MARGARET RENKL is a contributing opinion writer for *The New York Times*, where her essays appear weekly. Her work has also appeared in *Guernica*, *Literary Hub*, *Proximity*, and *River Teeth*, among others. She was the founding editor of *Chapter 16*, the daily literary publication of Humanities Tennessee, and is a graduate of Auburn University and the University of South Carolina. She lives in Nashville.

milkweed
editions

Founded as a nonprofit organization in 1980, Milkweed
Editions is an independent publisher. Our mission is to
identify, nurture and publish transformative literature,
and build an engaged community around it.

We are aided in this mission by generous individuals who
make a gift to underwrite books on our list. Special
underwriting for *Late Migrations* was provided by
Mary and Keith Bednarowski.

milkweed.org

Interior design by Mary Austin Speaker
Text typeset in Century; display set in Filosofia.

Century is a Scotch typeface originally cut by Linn Boyd
Benton for master printer Theodore Low De Vinne for use
in *Century* magazine. Later and more widely used iterations
of Century were redesigned by Benton's son, Morris Fuller
Benton, who devised the invention of type families.

Filosofia was designed by Zuzana Licko for Emigre in 1996 as
a contemporary interpretation of Bodoni.